Foundations of a Free Society

Foundations of a Free Society

EAMONN BUTLER

iea

The Institute of Economic Affairs

First published in Great Britain in 2013 by
The Institute of Economic Affairs
2 Lord North Street
Westminster
London SW1P 3LB
in association with Profile Books Ltd

The mission of the Institute of Economic Affairs is to improve public
understanding of the fundamental institutions of a free society, with particular
reference to the role of markets in solving economic and social problems.

A CIP catalogue record for this book is available from the British Library.

ISBN 978 0 255 36687 8
eISBN 978 0 255 36691 5

Many IEA publications are translated into languages other than English or
are reprinted. Permission to translate or to reprint should be sought from the
Director General at the address above.

Typeset in Stone by MacGuru Ltd
info@macguru.org.uk

Printed and bound in Britain by Hobbs the Printers

CONTENTS

	The author	8
	Foreword by Ali Salman	9
	Acknowledgements	12
	Summary	13
1	**Introduction**	17
	The purpose of this book	17
	How the book is set out	18
2	**The moral and economic benefits of freedom**	20
	A free society	20
	The moral case for freedom	24
	The economic case for freedom	31
3	**The institutions of a free society**	44
	Society without the state	44
	Why government must be limited	47
	Ways to limit government	58
	Setting the rules	64
4	**Equality and inequality**	67
	Equality in a free society	67
	Kinds of equality	68

Equality of outcome   75
Equality and justice   80
Further damage of egalitarianism   85

5 Free enterprise and trade   89
The free-market economy   89
How to grow rich   93
How markets work   99
International trade   105

6 Property and justice   110
Private property   110
The rules of justice   115
The rule of law   121
Human rights   126

7 The spontaneous society   130
Order without commands   130
Toleration   134
The problem of altruism   144

8 Privatisation and globalisation   150
Migration and technology   150
Growing a free society   151
Property rights in action   153
Human services without government   161
Globalisation and trade   168
The importance of peace   172

9 The argument in brief 175
The case for freedom 175
Limited government 175
Greater equality 176
A free economy 177
Justice and the rule of law 178
The spontaneous society 179
A world of freedom 179

Select bibliography 181

About the IEA 184

THE AUTHOR

Eamonn Butler is director of the Adam Smith Institute, a leading policy think tank. He has degrees in economics, philosophy and psychology, gaining a PhD from the University of St Andrews in 1978. During the 1970s he worked for the US House of Representatives, and taught philosophy at Hillsdale College, Michigan, before returning to the UK to help found the Adam Smith Institute. In 2012 he was awarded an Hon DLitt by the Edinburgh Business School. He is currently Secretary of the Mont Pelerin Society.

Eamonn is author of books on the pioneering economists Milton Friedman, F. A. Hayek and Ludwig von Mises, and a primer on the Austrian School of Economics. For the IEA, he has written primers on Adam Smith, Ludwig von Mises and public choice theory. He is co-author of a history of wage and price controls, and of a series of books on IQ. His recent popular publications, *The Best Book on the Market*, *The Rotten State of Britain* and *The Alternative Manifesto*, have attracted considerable attention, and he is a frequent contributor to print and broadcast media.

FOREWORD

Economic and political crises have often led to attacks on freedom. During the Great Depression all the major economies restricted trade by raising tariffs. This knee-jerk reaction only aggravated geo-political tensions and further increased economic hardship. The emergence of radical socialist regimes led to total oppression of civil, political and economic liberties in half the world.

More recently, the events of 9/11 and the US reaction have set in motion policies that have sacrificed freedom in an attempt to increase security. Similarly, the global financial crisis that began in 2008, and which was also germinated on US soil, has been followed by increasing controls, regulations and protections. Instead of relying on the creative destruction principle of free markets, governments on both sides of the Atlantic have used huge amounts of taxpayers' money to bail out failing businesses.

Threats to freedom abound. A quarter of a century ago, the world embraced 'glasnost' in the Soviet Union and then celebrated the fall of the Berlin Wall. But new challenges have now emerged in the form of neo-nationalism in Europe and radicalism in the Middle East. Both trends will reduce freedom if they go unchecked. In Europe, this reversion to nationalism, and even racism, is taking place despite a relatively high degree of political freedom – a functioning democracy exists. In the Middle East, the rise of religious radicalism is less surprising – neither market nor democracy is in good shape.

Despite these problems, individuals in the 21st century are in many respects freer than their predecessors in the previous century. The information and communication technology revolution has brought down all kinds of barriers. In China, for example, Li Chengpeng is a prominent writer and social critic: his Sina Weibo blog has nearly six million followers. And, during the Arab Spring, social media helped bring about widespread political and social progress. If information is power, then information technology has empowered the individual. Geographical boundaries remain, but they are becoming increasingly irrelevant.

In this context, the publication of Eamonn Butler's monograph could not be more timely. *Foundations of a Free Society* is a welcome addition to the family of modern primers on liberty. Butler's unique skill lies in his ability to express complex and highly influential ideas in plain English. He also successfully undermines the arguments of critics and opponents with real-world examples that illustrate his ideas and support the theoretical arguments.

This Occasional Paper is therefore an excellent introductory text for those who would like to understand the basic principles of a free society. It will be particularly helpful for those promoting freedom in countries where these principles remain largely unknown, as well as for those protecting freedom in places where traditional liberties are under assault.

ALI SALMAN

Founder and Executive Director,
Policy Research Institute of Market Economy (PRIME),
Islamabad, Pakistan
September 2013

The views expressed in this monograph are, as in all IEA publications, those of the author and not those of the Institute (which has no corporate view), its managing trustees, Academic Advisory Council members or senior staff. With some exceptions, such as with the publication of lectures, all IEA monographs are blind-peer-reviewed by at least two academics or researchers who are experts in the field.

ACKNOWLEDGEMENTS

Special thanks are due to Nigel Ashford, who has allowed the author to borrow heavily many ideas from his own book *Principles for a Free Society*. Other helpful sources have included H. B. Acton's *The Morals of Markets*, J. S. Mill's *On Liberty*, Madsen Pirie's *Freedom 101*, Richard Wellings's *A Beginner's Guide to Liberty*, Ernest Benn's *Why Freedom Works* and Tom Palmer's *The Morality of Capitalism*.

SUMMARY

- Freedom creates prosperity. It unleashes human talent, invention and innovation, creating wealth where none existed before. Societies that have embraced freedom have made themselves rich. Those that have not have remained poor.
- People in a free society do not become rich by exploiting others, as the elites of less-free countries do. They cannot become rich by making others poorer. They become rich only by providing others with what they want and making other people's lives better.
- The chief beneficiaries of the economic dynamism of free societies are the poor. Free societies are economically more equal than non-free societies. The poor in the most-free societies enjoy luxuries that were undreamed of just a few years ago, luxuries available only to the ruling elites of non-free countries.
- International trade gives entrepreneurs new market opportunities and has helped lift more than a billion people out of abject poverty in the last twenty years. Freedom is truly one of the most benign and productive forces in human history.
- Attempts by governments to equalise wealth or income are counter-productive. They destroy the incentives for hard work and enterprise and discourage people from building up the capital that boosts the productivity of the whole society.

- A free society is a spontaneous society. It builds up from the actions of individuals, following the rules that promote peaceful cooperation. It is not imposed from above by political authorities.
- Government has a very limited role in a free society. It exists to prevent harm being done to its citizens by maintaining and enforcing justice. It does not try to impose material equality and it does not prohibit activities just because some people consider them disagreeable or offensive. Leaders cannot plunder citizens for their own benefit, grant favours to their friends, or use their power against their enemies.
- The government of a free society is constrained by the rule of law. Its laws apply to everyone equally. There must be due process of law in all cases, with fair trials and no lengthy detention without trial. People accused of offences must be treated as innocent until proved guilty, and individuals must not be harassed by being prosecuted several times for the same offence.
- Tolerating other people's ideas and lifestyles benefits society. Truth is not always obvious; it emerges in the battle of ideas. We cannot trust censors to suppress only wrong ideas. They may mistakenly suppress ideas and ways of acting that would greatly benefit society in the future.
- Communications technology is making it more difficult for authoritarian governments to hide their actions from the rest of the world. As a result, more and more countries are opening up to trade and tourism, and new ideas are spreading. More people see the benefits of economic and social freedom, and are demanding them.

Foundations of a Free Society

1 INTRODUCTION

The purpose of this book

This book outlines the core principles that define a free society. The reason it is needed is because genuine personal, social, political and economic freedom is so rare – even in countries that think of themselves as being free. There are certainly big differences between the most-free and the least-free countries, yet in every country, to a greater or lesser extent, people's social and economic lives are restricted or controlled by officials and politicians. Such restrictions and controls have been around for so long, and restrain so much of our everyday lives, that they have become part of the very culture. People simply regard them as part of life, natural and inevitable.

The result is that much of the world's population, even if they believe they are living in a free society, can hardly imagine what real freedom means – still less understand what a free society might look like and how it could work.

Nevertheless, most people want freedom. They want to be able to trade without having to obtain countless permits. They want to be secure in their tenure of their homes, farms and workshops, rather than run the risk of politicians throwing them out and ruining them. They want to decide what is best for their own families rather than do what officials dictate. They want to get on with their lives without having to bribe police and bureaucrats to leave them alone.

That is why it is so important to map out the core principles of social and economic freedom. A clear vision of what freedom is, and how it works, is the foundation on which people can build a genuinely free society.

How the book is set out

Chapter 2 explains not just the *economic* benefits of having a free society, but the *moral* case for freedom too. A free economy and a free society are based on deep values – not values that challenge other moral systems but values that support, strengthen and enhance them. Freedom is for everyone.

Chapter 3 explains how a free society can provide people's needs smoothly and efficiently without needing powerful rulers telling everyone what to do. Indeed, it explains why government must be *limited* in scope and power, and it shows what a free society would look like and how it would work.

Chapter 4 discusses the apparent tension between *freedom* and *equality*. It argues that greater freedom in fact produces greater equality in everything that matters. But attempts to impose equality of outcome on a society undermine the principles of freedom and cause long-term damage.

Chapter 5 outlines the economic framework of a free society, explaining how markets, when freed from state control, create and spread prosperity. It explains the rules we follow to keep that process functioning smoothly, and the crucial importance of free trade in promoting human cooperation.

Chapter 6 examines the principles of *property* and *justice*. It explains how the laws of a free society must be general, applying to people in authority as much as to ordinary citizens, if coercion and exploitation are to be minimised. And it explains how a free society respects basic human rights.

Chapter 7 explains in more detail how a free society operates without needing to be commanded by those in authority. It outlines the basic *moral* and *behavioural rules* that establish a well-functioning but free social order. It stresses the need for *toleration*, and explains the problems of basing a society on altruism.

Chapter 8 looks at how to build a free society where none exists. It shows the importance of improving *incentives* in everyday life, and the folly of trying to impose decisions from above. It shows how even vital services can be provided without government. And it stresses the importance of *free trade* and *peace*.

2 THE MORAL AND ECONOMIC BENEFITS OF FREEDOM

A free society
What freedom means

Freedom (or liberty – the words are interchangeable in English) means more than simply not being imprisoned or enslaved. It means having the right to act, speak and think as you choose, without oppressive restrictions imposed on you by others, including those in authority. It applies in your personal, family and social life as well as to your political views and in your economic transactions with others.

A free society is one that seeks to uphold these ideals. Historically and today, freedom has proved remarkably successful at generating wealth and spreading it to citizens. It has proved to be one of humanity's most creative and productive forces. It has improved the lives of people – particularly the poorest people – around the globe.

Freedom means that no obstacles are put in your way, and no restraints prevent you from acting as you choose. It means not being coerced, directed, threatened, intimidated, pressurised, imposed on, interfered with or manipulated by others. It means being able to get on with your life without being attacked, defrauded, robbed or harmed. That is so because the principle of freedom applies equally to everyone in a free society. None of us has any right to interfere with, impede or harm others, which would negate the freedom that they also have.

So freedom exists only insofar as other people are not harmed. Your right to swing your fist ends where my nose begins. You are not exercising freedom if you threaten, coerce, rob, attack or murder others. On the contrary, you are curbing their freedom to go unmolested. This is called the 'no-harm' principle: *you are free to do whatever you want, provided that it does not harm others.*

Likewise, you are not curbing anyone's freedom by resisting their aggression. Freedom and the no-harm principle allow you to prevent others doing harm to you and those you cherish. You are also justified in intervening in order to prevent harm being done to anyone else, including strangers – although this function of protecting other citizens is often left to the police and legal authorities.

However, the no-harm principle applies only to harm done to *other people*. It allows you to do what you like with your own body and your own property, provided you do not violate the freedom of others in the process. For example, you can give away all your property, risk injury by doing something dangerous, or injure your own body, as long as none of this causes harm to anyone else. And although other people might well try to discourage this self-harm, they cannot physically stop you, if that is your deliberate choice.

Freedom and the role of government

It may seem harsh to say that we do not have the freedom to interfere in the actions of others, even if it is for their own good. But none of us can really know what is actually in the interests of others. Individuals are the best judges of their own welfare. They have a much closer understanding of their own values, circumstances, needs, wants, fears, hopes, aims and aspirations than anyone else. They are the best judges of their own goals and their own actions.

And outsiders might be biased in how they judge others. If we allow people to interfere with the freedom of others, they may do so in ways that (consciously or unconsciously) benefit themselves rather than the other person. This is why decisions about restraining others are left to the police and the judiciary, who – in a genuinely free society, at least – can be more objective in the matter.

Whoever we are, then, our individual ends are best served by being in a society where we are free. The role of government in such a society is to protect our freedom against violation by others – and to extend it to where it does not fully exist and enlarge it where it is incomplete. When people come together to form a government or any other authority over themselves, this is what they have in mind: to protect and expand their freedoms, not to restrict them.

All too often, though, governments are not created like this. They are imposed on the population by groups that are willing to use power to benefit their own interests, not to expand the freedom of everyone. Such predation often occurs with the full consent of the majority, who in turn gain from exploiting the minority. But freedom is not about numbers: to have any meaning at all, it has to apply equally to the whole population.

Even governments that do have the general interest at heart often diminish freedom because they do not fully understand or respect the no-harm principle, nor see the harm that their interventions cause. Government censors, for example, may forbid certain thoughts and words or pictures being spoken or broadcast, believing that these might cause public offence. But in the process they harm talented authors, artists, film-makers, journalists and others by curbing their freedom of thought and expression, thwarting their careers and denying them the fruits of their labour, creativity and intelligence. And once the principle of state censorship is accepted, it becomes too easy for those in power to extend it – forbidding any criticism of their government, say, or suppressing any ideas they find threatening.

Again, well-meaning authorities may impose taxes for the purpose of equalising incomes, overlooking how this removes the freedom of taxpayers to enjoy their own property as surely as ordinary theft does. And like ordinary theft, the threat of such confiscation is a sure way to prevent people from saving and investing – which in turn will have damaging effects on the security and prosperity of the whole population.

Such governments might claim to be acting in the public interest, but who is to know what the public interest is? Different people have different, and often competing, interests. Balancing those competing interests is an impossible job. But individuals are much better at knowing, and acting on, their own interests than are distant authorities who use official power to do it for them.

Coercion is an evil. And although some coercion – such as the restraint of aggressors – may be a necessary evil, we should still seek to reduce coercion to a minimum. Many advocates of freedom argue that all human beings have 'natural rights' – such as the right to life and the right to hold private property – which set the limits of government's power over us. We would not allow other citizens to rob or limit us, so why should we allow governments to do so?

For most of human history, however, people have not been free. Governments have not been set up by the voluntary agreement of individuals but imposed by those willing to use force. But no individual whose life is forcibly directed by some authority is a whole person. People are only morally complete if they make choices for themselves. They have little moral worth if others choose for them. For then they are mere ciphers, not entire human beings.

The moral case for freedom

Freedom allows people to become whole human beings by using their talents and abilities as they see fit – not just for themselves, but also for their families and others close to them. A free society is not a mass of isolated and self-interested individuals; it is a network of whole and social human persons. Its ability to help all of humanity underscores the moral dimension of a free society.

Spiritual and cultural roots of freedom

As the Nobel economist Amartya Sen has pointed out, freedom is a universal idea.[1] It has strong roots in almost all religions and cultures, from Islam to Buddhism, from Asia to the West. The Indian emperor Ashoka called for freedom and political tolerance more than twenty centuries ago. The sixteenth-century Mughul emperor Akbar was making classic observations on tolerance even as the Inquisition was persecuting religious dissidents in Europe. Islam, from its very earliest origins, was open to economic

---

1   Amartya Sen, 'Universal truths: human rights and the Westernizing illusion', *Harvard International Review*, 20(3), 1998, pp. 40–43.

freedom and enterprise long before these were respected in the West. The Turkish emperors were often more tolerant than European monarchs.

Freedom, in other words, is perfectly compatible with all the great cultures and religions of the world. It is not a particularly Western idea, nor a materialistic one, nor one at odds with a society based on strong social values. Indeed, a free society relies on people willingly accepting shared norms and rules that forbid harm, fraud, exploitation and the abuse of power – rules which help create a harmonious social order in which people can coexist and collaborate. Within that broad framework, freedom allows people to decide their own values, to maintain their own culture and to follow their own religious practices. They are not forced to accept the values, culture and practices of some state authority.

A culture of trust and cooperation

A free society does not operate on the basis of power and authority, but on a basis of trust and cooperation. Wealth in a free society comes through voluntary exchange, through people producing useful products and trading them with others. It does not come through the loot-and-grab tactics of predatory elites, using their power to extract taxes from the public or to grant monopolies and privileges to themselves, their family and their cronies. That may be how most wealth has been built up in most countries throughout human history – through exploitation based on coercive force. A free society depends instead on the much healthier motive of voluntary cooperation and exchange.

To work, voluntary cooperation and exchange requires *trust*. Nobody will trade with people they think are greedy swindlers

– unless they are forced to, or have no alternative (for example, where governments, or their cronies, control production). In a free society, people have a choice and are free to take their business elsewhere, so producers must convince customers – both present customers and potential future ones – that they are honest. They must deliver on their promises, or they will lose their reputation and go out of business. And for most people, a potential loss of reputation and livelihood is a serious concern.

A free society is not directed from above by elites using force. It works quite naturally and spontaneously through the voluntary interactions of ordinary people – bolstered by a culture of reliability and honesty. The rules and norms that drive this spontaneous cooperation become so natural in a free society that people do not even have to think about them. It does not require some authority to tell people to be honest and efficient, or to work hard and cooperate with others. People do this naturally every day.

The need for trust and cooperation in a free society makes the relationships between individuals and groups much more important than they are in power-directed societies. The ties of spiritual values, family, friendships, community, heritage, neighbourhood and associations of people with shared interests become more significant. Many governments in non-free societies regard such associations as a threat to their own authority, and have sought to weaken, subvert or abolish them. Usually they have succeeded only in driving groups underground. Voluntary association is so important to people that it is much stronger than people's loyalty to government authorities.

Self-interest and rules

A free society does not need orders from above. It works through ordinary individuals adjusting their own plans and actions to the plans and actions of other people. What enables them to do that is a simple set of shared rules and values – such as honesty and non-violence – that prevents conflict between different people with different personal interests.

Such basic rules and shared values do more than allow individuals to live in peace. They also leave people free to cooperate in order to advance their mutual interests. For example, a free society leaves people free to trade between each other, striking bargains that both sides consider beneficial. It is not up to some authority to decide what might benefit them, nor to decide how their different interests should be balanced, nor to decide what should be done to serve their interests, nor to compel people to follow that plan. In a free society, people themselves decide what is in their own interest, and choose how best to advance those interests by cooperating with other people. And they are free to enter into whatever bargains they choose, as long as no one else is harmed in the process.

Some critics cannot see how a society can function and prosper unless it chooses common goals and obliges all its citizens to work towards them. They fear that a free society would be a constant, unproductive, jarring clash of private ambitions – which must be suppressed to allow the public interest to prevail.

This is a mistake. A free society accepts that people are self-interested. But it accepts too that self-interest is such a strong motivation that it cannot easily be suppressed. People regard the 'public interest' – as defined by officials and politicians – as much less urgent and important than their own interests. And we must remember that self-interest is actually useful and important: if individuals neglected their own basic needs (such as food, drink, shelter and clothing), they would not survive very long, no matter how charitable the society they live in.

A free society channels self-interest in beneficial ways. It does not suppress it in the vain hope of creating some utopia. A set of rules requires only that people do not impose their own ambitions on others. People are free to pursue their own interests, individually or in partnership with others, as long as they respect the freedom of others to do the same. They cannot force others to accept and serve their own particular goals.

The critics' fear that a free society would be a perpetual war of competing interests is undermined by the fact that relatively free societies do prosper – and nearly always prosper better than more controlled ones. Using a set of simple rules under which people respect the freedoms of others, they channel self-interest into useful cooperation and collaboration.

The fear that individuals in a free society would think only about advancing their own interests is similarly mistaken. Human beings are social creatures. They have a natural affinity with family, friends and neighbours, whose interests they take account of in their actions. They crave the respect and goodwill of friends, and the reputation of being a good neighbour. So they willingly temper their own interests in order to maintain good relations with others. Their consideration is rewarded, because then others will be more likely to help them in return.

We can see this working in the more-free societies. Giving to others, even complete strangers, through private philanthropy is much greater in the more-free societies than in the less-free ones – not just because people there are more wealthy, but because free societies put greater emphasis on voluntary, rather than imposed, social obligations.

Cooperation through agreed rules

To cooperate successfully with others, we each need to make our actions predictable and reliable. Cooperation would be impossible if people constantly changed their minds, acted in random ways or reneged on promises. A free society allows people to behave as they choose in their personal lives, provided that others are not harmed. But it also encourages the sort of consistency in behaviour that is essential in social cooperation.

For example, a free society has *legal rules* about the ownership, control and transference of property. This allows people to acquire property and to invest in capital goods – such as houses, factories and equipment that will improve their future lives and make production easier and cheaper – without the threat of being robbed or exploited by other people or by officials. These rules ('property rights') have not been designed by governments, but have simply grown up over the centuries. Their limits have been tested in countless disputes in countless courts, building up a body of law and practice that makes people more secure in their dealings with others – and so makes cooperation easier and more fruitful.

The more-free societies have also come to accept many other rules and norms as essential to harmonious social cooperation. *Moral rules* set limits that help make social interaction easier for everyone. And there are general *standards of social behaviour* – manners, politeness and norms of good business practice – which grow up gradually over a long period of human interactions. Such beneficial norms, though commonplace in the more-free societies, can be hard or impossible for the governments of less-free countries to reproduce.

Citizens of a free society also have certain basic *civil rights*. Their exact form may vary, but these accepted norms include freedom from forced labour or slavery, and freedom from torture or disproportionate punishments for offences. They include freedom of conscience and belief – the freedom to hold your own ideas about religion or politics, the freedom to practise your own religion and to take part in politics without threats or intimidation. They include freedom of speech – the freedom to express oneself and the freedom of the communications media (radio, television, newspapers and internet providers) to report and comment as they choose. They include the freedom to assemble and associate with whom you wish. And they include privacy – not being spied on and monitored by others, especially those in authority. In short, a free society expects its citizens to be tolerant of people's views, beliefs, lifestyle and actions, and not to intervene in them, subject to the no-harm rule.

Justice and the rule of law

A free society also has *rules of justice*. There are penalties for harming other people, not just physical harm but fraud and other harm too. And, perhaps most importantly, a free society upholds the rule of law. The main problem of political organisation is not how to choose our leaders – that is easy – but how to *restrain* them. In a free society, the role and power of government authorities are strictly limited. This ensures that the power given to them to defend citizens from aggression and to punish wrongdoing is not used arbitrarily or for the self-interest of those who wield it.

Free societies have developed all sorts of different mechanisms – such as election law, constitutions and the separation of powers – in order to restrain official power. But the key way to protect citizens against exploitation by their rulers is to make sure that laws apply equally to everyone. This is known as the *rule of law*. Under this principle, a government could not vote favours or privileges to particular tribes, for example, nor impose taxes on particular social groups. And the laws have to apply to the government itself as well as to the public.

The same applies to the enforcement of those laws. In order to make sure that judicial power is used dispassionately and not arbitrarily, the rules of justice apply equally in a free society. Citizens are entitled to equal treatment and due processes of justice. That includes not being subjected to arbitrary arrest, not being imprisoned without trial, a fair trial conducted according to rules of evidence, judgement made by a jury of ordinary citizens rather than appointed officials, and not being subjected to trial after trial for the same offence.

The effect of all these limits on politicians, officials and judges is to erode the abuse of power by those in authority, to undermine special privileges and to reduce the evil of coercion. After all, the role of government in a free society is to protect and extend the freedom of individuals, not to diminish it.

The economic case for freedom
The huge rise in living standards

Until the 1750s, human life did not change very much. Nearly everyone worked outdoors on the land, in the laborious, uncertain, weather-beaten activity of cultivating food. The methods of that agriculture were much the same as they were back in the days of the pharaohs. Most people had no money for luxuries such as a spare set of clothing. Few could afford meat. The only conspicuously rich people were those who were born into wealth. And usually, that wealth originated with the power to tax the peasant population for your own gain – or from being a servant or friend of someone who had that power.

It was, for most people, a miserable existence. In 1800, calculates the economist Deirdre McCloskey, the income of the average world citizen was somewhere between $1 and $5 a day – hardly enough for a cup of coffee in most of the world's capitals today.[2] Now, average world earnings are nearer to $50 a day. That is a huge rise in prosperity.

But even that is only an average, which masks the prosperity that some countries – though not others – have been able to achieve. Average earnings in Tajikistan, one of the least-free countries in the world, remain little more than $7 a day. But average earnings in the United States, one of the most free, are now over $100 a day. Thanks to the benefits of freedom, Americans today are fourteen times richer than people in Tajikistan, and between 20 and 100 times richer than their ancestors were in 1800. In Switzerland, Australia, Canada and the United Kingdom – all ranked by *The Economic Freedom of the World Report* as among the world's most-free countries – average earnings are more than $90 a day. Freedom and prosperity go together.[3]

It is no surprise, therefore, that people are leaving the poor,

2 Deirdre N. McCloskey, 'Liberty and dignity explain the modern world', in Tom G. Palmer (ed.), *The Morality of Capitalism*, Students for Liberty and Atlas Foundation, Arlington, VA, 2011.

3 Fraser Institute, *Economic Freedom of the World 2012 Annual Report*, Fraser Institute, Vancouver, BC, 2012.

less-free countries and migrating to the rich, more-free ones. Each year, the 20 least-free countries see roughly 1.12 more people per 1,000 population moving out than moving in. By contrast the 20 most-free countries see 3.81 per 1,000 more people moving in than moving out.[4] And the most economically free of those 20 see the highest net immigration. On average, countries in the bottom half of the freedom scale are losing migrants, while those in the top half are gaining them.

In other words, people are voting for freedom with their feet. And they are doing so despite the best efforts of the non-free countries to prevent people emigrating and of the more-free countries to restrict immigration.

Freedom and philanthropy

It is not exploitation of their own poor which makes the free countries rich. As the Russian moral philosopher Leonid Nikonov has observed, the average *share* of national income going to the poorest tenth of the population in the most-free and least-free countries was almost identical (2.58 per cent and 2.47 per cent respectively). But it remains far better to be poor in a rich country (where the poorest tenth earn an average $23 a day) than to be poor in a poor country (where the poorest tenth earn just $2.50 a day).[5]

Wealth in the free, rich countries is also more accessible to people. Their poorest citizens are not permanently excluded from

---

4   Gabriel Openshaw, 'Free markets and social welfare', *Mises Daily*, 4 October 2005, http://www.mises.org/daily/1915#_edn2.

5   Leonid Nikonov, 'The moral logic of equality and inequality in market society', in Tom G. Palmer (ed.), *The Morality of Capitalism*, Students for Liberty and Atlas Foundation, Arlington, VA, 2011.

making themselves rich – unlike those in less-free countries who do not happen to come from the right family, caste, race or religion, or political group. There is much greater social mobility in the more-free countries. The world's richest man, Microsoft founder Bill Gates, famously started his software business in a garage.

And now, Gates is aiming to give away all his fortune to good causes. That is entirely typical: private philanthropy too is much greater in richer countries. A survey by Barclays Wealth found that two-fifths of the wealthiest Americans report *charitable giving* as one of their top three spending priorities.[6]

According to the UK's Charities Aid Foundation, the five countries in which people are most likely to donate money and time to philanthropic causes are Australia, Ireland, Canada, New Zealand and the United States – all ranking high in terms of freedom.[7] And those countries all have more wealth to give away than do the citizens of poor, less-free countries.

Freedom thwarts discrimination

In non-free countries, discrimination is rife. It can be hard to get a good job, or access to good services, if you are not of the right class, caste, religion, sex or family. But free-market economies squeeze out discrimination. Producers in free societies cannot afford to discriminate when choosing with whom to trade or who to hire.[8]

Employers, for example, might dislike immigrants, especially

6   Barclays Wealth, *Global Giving: The Culture of Philanthropy*, London, 2010.

7   Charities Aid Foundation, *World Giving Index 2012*, Charities Aid Foundation, West Malling, 2012.

8   For a good outline of this point, see Milton Friedman and Rose Friedman, *Capitalism and Freedom*, University of Chicago Press, Chicago, IL, 1962.

Question: Aren't free societies just crassly materialistic?
No. Economic freedom gives people choices and opportunities. It provides their basic needs – food, shelter and clothing – far better. And it gives them opportunities that were undreamed of before the rise of free trade and markets. Instead of condemning people to a lifetime of hard and degrading work, it allows people to enjoy things they consider more uplifting, such as travel, music, art, culture and social activities. It enables them to afford proper healthcare and better education.

Wealth is just a tool that gives us access to what we truly value – not just our material comfort, but also what we value culturally and socially. That is why the richer, more-free countries have more sports stadia, concert halls, theatres, universities, libraries and museums.

if they come from a different culture, race or religion. But immigrant groups can – and often do – respond by accepting lower wages for the same work. Then, employers who discriminate by hiring only native workers will find themselves at a competitive disadvantage. Their wage bills will be higher than those of competitors who are willing to hire immigrants. Their profits will be lower, or they will have to charge higher prices and risk losing trade. That is bad for business. It is simply not in the commercial interests of employers to discriminate.

Even within the domestic workforce, the free-market economy squeezes out discrimination. For example, there may be cultural opposition against women going out to work, making it harder for them to get a job. But employers who do discriminate against women will have a much smaller pool of talent to draw on than their competitors who do not. Another interesting example is the caste divide in India. The rise of high-tech industries in centres such as Hyderabad has greatly boosted the employment prospects of lower-caste Indian workers. Employers in this competitive industry need people for their brainpower. They cannot afford to discriminate on caste, or any other cultural factor. What anti-discrimination laws have failed to achieve in decades, the simple self-interest of free business people is achieving in a few years.

The creativity of a free people

One reason why the more-free economies are richer is that they use all available talent. With less discrimination to thwart them, all citizens of a free society are free to put their minds and abilities to work. If they create, improve and supply products that make other people's lives better, those people will reward them by buying their products. So free societies are more creative and innovative, and therefore develop faster.

Economic freedom channels people's self-interest in socially beneficial directions. You earn money by producing what other people want and are willing to pay you for. And you want them to come back for more, and to tell all their friends how good you are. That focuses producers very much on their customers rather than themselves. Most of the well-known business people in the more-free societies say that they have made their businesses successful by attending to the wants and needs of their customers, rather than by trying to extract more profit from them.

This reality is very distant from the 'dog eat dog' caricature of free economies. A genuinely free economy is a hugely cooperative system, based not on coercion but on voluntary trade and exchange between free people.

The creation of capital

As well as encouraging innovation and customer service, free economies become rich through building up productive capital. It is much easier to catch fish with a net than by hand, but this means catching fewer fish for a time while you labour on making your net. By forgoing consumption, you can build up capital, and make future production much more efficient.

This is the basis of capitalism. People build up capital, such as houses, factories and machinery, that makes their lives easier and their labour more productive (often very much more productive: think of the difference in effort involved in cultivating farmland with tractors, rather than with hand ploughs). And the process is cumulative: each addition and improvement to productive technology boosts production and reduces effort even more.

A free society can accumulate this productive capital and keep on increasing its productivity and its prosperity only because it gives people the ability to own houses, factories, machinery and other capital goods without fear of them being confiscated or stolen. It defends people against confiscation, and it has moral and legal rules about property ownership that make theft less likely.

This protection of property ownership, through law and culture, is a hugely important feature of a free society and a free economy. After all, few farmers are likely to go to the effort of seeding, planting out, cultivating and nurturing crops if they believe that their harvest is likely to be stolen by bandits. Likewise, few people are likely to work more than they have to if most of their income is taken in taxes. Families will not save if they are cheated out of their money by the stealth tax of inflation. Entrepreneurs are unlikely to invest in their businesses if their assets might be nationalised without compensation. Privileges that skew the market to benefit favoured elites make it less likely that anyone else will try to grow new businesses.

And the greater this exploitation by thieves or governments, the greater is the disincentive against work, saving and progress. Ibn Khaldun, the fourteenth-century Islamic scholar and jurist, understood the point very well. He wrote:

> It should be known that attacks on people's property remove the incentive to acquire and gain property. People then become of the opinion that the purpose and ultimate destiny of acquiring property is to have it taken away from them. When the incentive to acquire and obtain property is gone, people no longer make efforts to acquire any. The extent and degree to which property rights are infringed upon determines the extent and degree to which the efforts of the subjects to acquire property slacken.[9]

Property and progress

But being secure in your ownership of property gives you a stake in your own future and that of your family. For example, if you are able to own your own home – which in many countries most people cannot – you have somewhere safe from which to run your life. You also have an asset against which you can borrow in order to start a business and build up your own productive capital, instead of being forever at the mercy of the rich elite. It gives you a financial cushion that allows you to experiment with new things – say, to quit your job and look for another, or to finance a new business venture.

---

9   Ibn Khaldun, *Muqaddimah: An Introduction to History*, 1377.

Secure property ownership promotes specialisation and trade, which increase human productivity and so adds to human wealth. Our lives would be very poor if we had to do everything for ourselves – grow our own food, fetch our own water, forage for our own fuel, make our own clothes, build our own houses or defend ourselves against attack. Few of us have the skills to do all these things, and we would need the right tools to do them all with any ease and efficiency. But if people's ownership of property is respected, we do not have to do everything ourselves. People can build up the specialist tools they need to do one task very efficiently, and then sell their products to the rest of us. The farmer can invest in ploughs and tractors, the house builder in ladders and shovels, the dressmaker in looms and sewing machines. And they can become far more skilled in their own profession, and better managers of their production, than all-round self-sufficient amateurs could ever hope to be. Through this *division of labour* we all enjoy better-quality products, lower costs and much more bountiful lives.

But again, this is possible only if people are secure enough to build up productive capital and engage in trade, confident that they will not be robbed or cheated. The alternative is grim. As Ibn Khaldun went on: 'When people no longer do business in order to make a living, and when they cease all gainful activity, the business of civilisation slumps, and everything decays. People scatter everywhere in search of sustenance, to places outside the jurisdiction of their present government.' That is a something that is all too clear today as we see the migration from the non-free to the more-free countries.

Creating wealth at nobody's expense

Some people imagine that one person's property can come only at the expense of someone else. This is not so. A free economy actually *creates* property and *adds value* to existing property.

Value is not a physical quality of things. It is what people *think* of things. Sellers part with goods because they value them less than their customers' cash. Customers part with cash because they value the goods they buy more than the money they pay for them. Even schoolchildren will swap toys, each reckoning they benefit by exchanging something they have grown tired of for something they want. Their exchange has created value. Nobody is left worse off by such trade: indeed, neither side would accept the deal if they thought they would lose by it.

Similarly, if someone plants seed and grows crops where none were before, and other people are willing to pay for that produce, they are creating new value out of something that was previously unproductive. Wealth has been created, but nobody has been robbed.

And again, if an entrepreneur builds a factory to make shoes, or clothes or cars or some new invention that people are willing to buy – and makes money out of the process – who is robbed? They might accumulate a fortune, but they have stolen nothing from anyone. On the contrary, they have created and spread value where none existed before.[10]

A free society is not crony capitalism

Some people argue that in capitalism, rich corporate interests

---

10   This point is well made by UK businessman Sir Ernest Benn in *Why Freedom Works*, Sir Ernest Benn Ltd, London, 1964.

exploit the poor, and politicians steal wealth from the masses by giving monopolies, privileges, grants and subsidies to their business friends.

But in a genuinely free society, competition makes exploitation and 'crony capitalism' impossible. Businesses depend on customers for their very existence. If they do not deliver a good service, those customers will desert them for other suppliers. And there will always be other potential suppliers because in a free society governments do not have the power to create monopolies, protect particular companies, or prevent people growing new businesses. A genuinely free economy produces competition, which empowers consumers over producers: companies will go out of business if they do not produce the value-for-money products that people want. Some companies might well grow very large – for example, in sectors such as car production, which requires a big capital investment. But they still face actual or potential competition from other large investors who think they can do better. The problems begin only when the authorities stifle competition and discourage or prevent new competitors from coming in.

Certainly, genuinely open competition is hard to maintain. Even in the most-free societies of the world today, politicians impose rules and regulations that – often unintentionally – reduce competition and so weaken the power that consumers have over producers. And producers all too often conspire in bringing this about. For example, established companies may press politicians to bring in regulations over product quality and manufacturing standards, specifying what can be produced and how. They may argue that these rules are needed to protect the public from shoddy goods. But the real result is to protect their business against new or smaller suppliers who may produce innovative products in innovative ways that are not listed in the regulations. Or again, politicians may intervene to use public money to shore up industries that are facing bankruptcy or are threatened by foreign competition, arguing that domestic jobs need to be protected. They might even ban foreign imports to protect the domestic industry. That might bring temporary relief to those who work in those industries – but at a cost to taxpayers and the public, who then have less choice and face paying more than they should have to for poorer-quality goods.

The more that a society drifts away from freedom and instead grants economic power to authorities, the more scope there is for producers and politicians to conspire to exploit people for their own benefit. Traces of such crony capitalism are found everywhere, but the problem is far worse in the least-free economies. Often, it is simply taken for granted that those who achieve power will use it to enrich themselves and their families and friends. It may even be thought a sign of weakness if they do not.

But in a genuinely free society authorities are not allowed to use legislative power or taxpayer funds to grant special economic privileges to cronies. There are strict rules on how power is wielded and where public funds are spent. Producers cannot successfully lobby those in authority to get subsidies and protections, since the power to grant those favours simply does not exist.

What gives companies and politicians the power to exploit ordinary people is a lack of freedom, not competitive capitalism.

The triumph of freedom

Though economic freedom and trade are rarely completely free, they have still managed to raise perhaps two billion people out of the most abject poverty over the last 30 years. That is something that the centralised and powerful governments of Russia, China and South-East Asia never achieved, despite half a century of trying. But as walls and trading barriers have fallen, more and more countries have entered the global trade system, and wealth has spread. It has spread particularly to the very poorest people in the very poorest countries that have embraced the new freedom to trade internationally. Can there be a more benign and productive principle on the planet than freedom?

3 THE INSTITUTIONS OF A FREE SOCIETY

Society without the state
Freedom and culture

In a free society, a large part of people's lives is lived in the complete absence of government. This is not just a case of the old Indian joke: 'The economy grows at night – when the government is sleeping'. Rather it is that government has no role at all in most of the activities that are really important to people.

People in a free society are not isolated individuals. On the contrary, they are social creatures. They seek out the company of others, try to fit in with others, and collaborate with others in many ways. They may be active members of religious groups. In clubs and societies they associate with others who enjoy the same things that they do, whether it is singing, reading, cooking, fishing, playing and watching sports or collecting. They associate and form groups with others like themselves, whether they are young, old, school friends, new parents, or people with similar disabilities. They may run soup kitchens or hostels for needy and homeless people. This is what is called *civil society*.

And despite the freedom of action and of movement that people enjoy in more-free societies, their citizens mostly share and respect common values, cultures and traditions. Free individuals, especially the young, may sometimes challenge the old ways – and indeed that is how better ways of doing things are discovered and progress is made. But freedom is not the enemy of culture. Even immigrants who do not share a particular culture must at least *respect* the prevailing culture if they are to be accepted into society. They may need to learn the language if they are to secure employment. And while they may not at first understand the traditions and moral principles of their adopted country, they will have to do so quickly if they are to avoid offence, and are to prosper. It is not that they would be actively discriminated against: in a free society, people are treated equally. But nobody in the native population – or any other – has to seek out the company of others who they find disagreeable, or who do not respect their ways or who cannot properly communicate with them.

Human beings desire company, and need it as a way of securing opportunities and advancing their own interests. So being an outsider puts you at a big disadvantage. People in a free society may not all share each other's values, but in simple human terms, it pays to tolerate them. The freedom of thought and speech and action that people have in a free society necessarily pays respect to the prevailing culture, morality and traditions.

Who needs government?

This informal web of mutual interest, collaboration, obligation, trust and reliance greatly enhances our lives. But it does not need government for it to function. We cooperate with each other, and prosper through our membership of various groups, without any authorities getting involved.

Even in the field of law, which one might think was unarguably a government function, we decide most things between ourselves.

Contracts in a free society are not designed and imposed by the state but drawn up by the parties concerned, who outline the terms they are prepared to accept and agree to them voluntarily. Those who do enter into contracts often agree to have any disputes between them judged by independent arbitration rather than the state-run courts, which can be much slower, much more expensive and much less fair than the private alternative.

It helps the creation of such informal and cooperative social relationships if the population itself is fairly homogenous. If most people come from the same race or religion, they will share values and find it easier to enter into agreements with confidence. That has not been helped by colonial regimes and post-war international conferences that have redrawn traditional boundaries and lumped different ethnic groups together. Many countries recently torn apart by conflict, such as Syria, Libya, Lebanon or Iraq, did not exist a century ago; they are the creations of politicians, not of peoples. The British made similar mistakes in Africa and the Indian subcontinent, lumping together different tribal or ethnic groups in the same administrative colony.

No wonder that we have so many fragile states, in which governments cannot even protect the lives and property of their citizens. That is stony ground on which to grow a free society and free economy. It is not easy to re-create a cooperative culture once it has been shattered and there are no bonds of mutual respect and trust on which to base our cooperation. The best that can be hoped for is that the different groups can draw up settlements that allow them to coexist, even if they do not properly cooperate together. But coexistence and cooperation between different peoples will always be much easier if the conditions of a free society are established, with the prospect of mutual benefit resulting.

Why government must be limited

What should government do?

Few people today believe that government should control every part of our lives. We all believe that the role of government should be limited in some way. Most people accept that we need government to decide or do things that have to be decided or done collectively, but that it should not interfere in things that we can do perfectly well by ourselves. And most thinking people conclude that there should be restraints on our leaders to prevent them overstepping their authority.

The issue is not so much the *size* of government, but *what* it is there to decide and do, and *how* it decides and does these things. Since a free society and its economy are based on trust, the citizens of free societies naturally expect their government to protect them against fraud and theft. But we would not wish the authorities to give people life imprisonment for dodging a bus fare, nor install spy cameras in everyone's home in case they are illicitly downloading music from internet sharing sites. Government action must be proportionate to the problem.

Another reason why government should be limited in its scope is that decisions made by individuals – over whether to trade a particular good, say – are purely voluntary. But decisions made by government – say to *stop* people from trading in a particular good – require the use of force to be effective. The use of force is an evil, even if it is sometimes necessary. When we make decisions politically, we should balance the benefit they achieve against the evil of the force they rest on. We should not rush to pursue the benefit without thinking of the harm.

And economic and social life both need freedom in order to grow. They develop through a gradual process of small-scale trial and error. Countless innovators try many different ideas – a new product, for example, or a new teaching method. The ideas that do not work are soon abandoned, but those that improve life are copied and spread by other people. But government control of economic and social institutions denies innovators any scope: the constant but gradual process of trial and error is slowed.

Furthermore, when governments intervene, it is generally on a big scale. They make decisions for the whole population on issues such as what products are to be manufactured or what teaching methods are to be adopted. Inevitably, this slows innovation and progress too. And when governments make mistakes – as inevitably they will – they are huge, catastrophic mistakes.

Why have government at all?

There are still good reasons to have governments doing certain things. We might need an authority to decide and enforce some essential rules about how we act – deciding which side of the road we drive on, for example, or making sure that we honour our contracts.

In addition, there may be some projects that it is in everyone's interest to have done, but which are unlikely to be done (or done well) by any individual. These are the so-called *public goods*. Defence and policing might be examples: while everyone benefits from improved security, why should anyone volunteer to serve? Another example is the air pollution that chokes the air of cities in many developing countries. Using smokeless fuels for heating, fitting catalytic converters to cars, and installing waste filters on factory chimneys might help cure the problem and make life better all round. But people will not volunteer for the expense of doing that, when they know that everyone else could simply 'free-ride' on their sacrifice, and enjoy cleaner air at their expense. So instead we may decide such issues politically, and force everyone to curb their pollution, or tax everyone to pay for police and security. Then we achieve things that produce widespread benefits, but which the market does not deliver.

Some proponents of freedom – we might call them *libertarians* – would argue that we do not need government at all. They say that free societies are extremely good at finding ways to cooperate and ways to deliver benefits to everyone, for example by means of philanthropic giving, or by finding clever ways to discourage free-riding by limiting benefits to people who pay. They are not even convinced that we need governments to enforce contracts or protect our lives from attack and our property from theft, thinking that individuals or groups can do all these well enough for themselves.

Other advocates of a free society – *classical liberals* – argue that at least some political decision-making, and some government power, is needed to protect us, to enforce agreements and to deliver public goods – though it should be limited to these functions. Libertarians, however, still fear that if you give governments an inch they will take a mile: nearly all the world's governments today have found roles for themselves – at the public's expense – that go well beyond these core functions.

Views on personal and economic freedom

Deciding on how far the role of government should extend is not a simple matter of 'left' versus 'right'. People disagree not only on whether decisions should be made by *individuals* or *collectively*,

Question: Surely government must provide things like defence?

No. There are certainly some things that must be *decided* collectively, such as whether to go to war, but there are very few things that cannot be *provided* privately. Many countries contract at least some of their defence functions to private companies, which make the vehicles, ships, aircraft and equipment, build and maintain the barracks, and provide the food and logistics.

It was not long ago that we used to think that only governments could deliver the mail, run the telephone system, operate the railways, provide water, gas and electricity, build roads, hospitals and prisons, or even produce steel and make cars. Now private firms do all these things. And, because they face competition, the quality they have to produce is higher.

but also on whether that should apply to both our *personal* and our *economic* decisions.

We might identify four different viewpoints.

- The first group we might call *individualists*. They hold that individuals should be free to make their own decisions about both their *personal* and *economic* lives.
- Diametrically opposite are the *authoritarians*, who advocate collective control over both *personal* and *economic* behaviour.
- The third group is those who advocate individual freedom in *economic* decisions but collective authority over people's *personal* choices. They might be called *conservatives* (though the term means different things in different cultures). This

mixture of economic freedom but social control is a common feature of many Asian countries.

- The last group is those who want collective control over *economic* life but who would leave individuals to run their *personal* lives.

It is particularly hard to find a good name for this last group. In the United States, they would be called *liberals*, but this is a very misleading use of the word. In most other countries, *liberal* means *classical liberal* – the idea that some framework of government rules is needed, but that most economic and personal decisions should be left up to individuals. In effect, the term has been stolen by American politicians and intellectuals who believe in personal freedom but who want government to have more control over economic life.

All these one-word descriptions are rather inexact ways of describing what is in reality a spectrum of views about economic and social issues. There is a wide range of views even within each group. (The *individualists*, for example, range from the *libertarians*, who would argue for total freedom, to the *classical liberals*, who see a limited role for government. The *authoritarians*, meanwhile, range from *totalitarians*, advocating total control, to *statists* who see a limited role for private decision-making.)

Nevertheless, it is useful to be aware that political views cannot adequately be described on a simple 'left–right' spectrum, which would lump together people with quite different views of society. It is more useful to think about it in terms of how much freedom people think there should be across two different parts of life, the *economic* and the *personal*.

Why individual choice?

There are strong reasons to prefer freedom in both economic and personal life. For a start, people know their own needs much better than distant governments ever could. They feel their own hopes, fears, dreams, desires, needs, wants and ambitions. They are much more aware of their own circumstances and those of the friends, family and communities they cherish and seek to help. They know much better the opportunities that are open to them, and the problems that different actions might cause. So they are in by far the best position to make decisions about their own lives and future.

There is also the moral point that people whose decisions are made for them are not whole human beings but mere slaves. And having no personal responsibility for what happens, they never learn from their successes and mistakes. They may suffer the evils of bad policy made by the authorities, but can do little to prevent it happening again, so see no reason to try. But individuals who enjoy the benefits of their successes, and suffer the costs of their mistakes, are strongly motivated to repeat what works and avoid what does not.

Diversity promotes progress

There is also advantage in diversity. People who are free to make their own decisions will act in a variety of different ways. They can choose the actions that they think are right for their own circumstances. They can try out different lifestyles – 'experiments in living', as the English philosopher John Stuart Mill called it in his 1859 essay 'On liberty'.[1] Some of these may be successful,

---

1   John Stuart Mill, 'On liberty', 1859, in John Stuart Mill, *On Liberty and Other Essays*, Oxford University Press, Oxford, 2008.

others not. But we can all learn from them, and advance our own progress, doing more of what seems to work and less of what does not.

In an authoritarian society, by contrast, only one way of doing things prevails because the decisions are made collectively. Any mistakes are catastrophic for everyone. And even if the official approach succeeds, we are not allowed to try other things that might work even better. Decision-making will be slower and more bureaucratic. Our progress in such a world will be slow and often painful.

In a free economy, producers get continual feedback from their customers. Every moment of every day, people are choosing the products they prefer over others. They are constantly weighing up price, reliability, size, shape, colour and scores of other qualities for each and every product they buy. Those diverse preferences are instantly transmitted to producers, who see what sells and what does not. Mindful that their competitors are doing the same, suppliers will move as fast as they can to produce more of what people want, and less of what they do not. And they will be stimulated to experiment with introducing new and different products that they hope customers will like even more.

Contrast that, again, with an economy where the authorities decide what is produced. It does not matter whether they control the whole economy, or just certain parts of it, as is usually the case: decision-making about what should be produced and how will still be a slow and clumsy business. At best, customers may be able to express their choices every few years, at elections. But they will not be voting on individual products and qualities: if they get a real choice at all they will be voting on a whole package of policies that might include everything from defence, schooling and healthcare to irrigation, agriculture and rural transport. The authorities have nothing like the constant, incentivising feedback that customers give suppliers in a market economy. There is little pressure on the authorities to innovate, and consumers do not get what they really want.

Depressive effects of intervention

There are few countries today where the government runs – or even tries to run – the entire production of the nation. Much more common is that governments control specific sectors – particularly those seen as essential, such as healthcare, education, agriculture or policing – or that they try to steer production more generally through subsidies, price caps and regulations on businesses.

Even when governments try to run just a few sectors, the problems of slow and clumsy decision-making remain, especially where these sectors are the ones of most critical importance. The government might run only the production of food, for example: but if it fails to produce sufficient quantities of the food that people need, the result could be widespread famine.

Likewise, government efforts to steer production more generally produce the same mismatch of supply and demand. For example, politicians may try to keep down the prices of some goods or services – food, say, or healthcare, or interest rates – by imposing price caps on them. But producers then earn less from supplying these things. The price they get does not justify the effort they spend on production. So they produce less, or leave the sector entirely.

The result is shortages. At the artificially low prices imposed by law, producers will supply less, but consumers will want to buy more. Food may officially be cheap, but there is none on the shelves; interest rates may be low but loans are impossible to find; healthcare may be free but you have to queue up to get it.

There are similar problems when governments try to steer production by subsidising the production of particular goods or services. The European Union, for example, has long subsidised and protected its farming sector, supposedly to ensure a strong and continual supply of food, but in fact to protect inefficient European farmers against international competition (and to buy the support of this politically important group). Subsidies encouraged massive over-production – with 'mountains' of unwanted butter and 'lakes' of unsold wine.

But there are other consequences, less visible than these. The biggest gainers from Europe's agricultural subsidies have been the biggest landowners, not the poorest farmers. And corruption has been rife, with farmers claiming subsidies for food that they never produced. There are countless similar stories from around the world, and indeed from history: in his 1776 book *The Wealth of Nations*, the Scottish economist Adam Smith complained of herring boats being equipped so as to maximise their subsidies rather than their catch.[2]

Subsidising any form of production draws resources to that sector and away from others where time, effort and capital might be employed better. For example, many governments are currently subsidising expensive wind and solar power, taking money from individuals and businesses that could find much more cost-effective ways of investing it. That is a drag on economic growth that depresses the long-term prosperity of the public.

---

2   Adam Smith, *The Wealth of Nations*, 1776, Book IV, ch. V.

Decisions by the few

Another reason to prefer decision-making by individuals rather than by the authorities is that choices are made by the many rather than by a powerful few. Inevitably, the authorities that make the decisions for everyone will need to have the power to put their decisions into effect. But the authorities are also human beings; and it is asking too much of them to resist the temptation to use that power to promote their own interests and those of their family or friends or neighbourhood or clan or political party. Contracts and monopolies are awarded to their associates. A disproportionate amount of public spending goes to senior politicians' home districts. Jobs in government, the police and the judiciary go to favourites, instead of being awarded on merit.

But the less that is decided politically, and the more by individuals themselves, the less scope there is for this kind of corruption. Government can be focused on its primary role of minimising coercion – rather than profiting from it.

Sometimes the profiteering is too subtle to see. 'There is no art which one government sooner learns of another', wrote the father of modern economics Adam Smith, 'than that of draining money from the pockets of the people.'[3] By borrowing, for example, governments can spend on projects that win them elections and enrich their supporters, while passing the cost on to others. They can even pass the cost to the next generation. If their debt gets too daunting, they can simply print money and repay their creditors in devalued currency. But such theft, open or hidden, discourages people from building up wealth. They become less likely to start new businesses and build up productive capital, and the whole society is made worse off.

---

3   Ibid., Book V, ch. II, Part II, Appendix to Articles I & II.

The government of a truly free society would not be permitted to borrow except in extreme situations, and even that would be limited. Nor would it have a monopoly over the currency and be able to print more when it needed money. And taxes in a free society would be low and levied on a broad base – not heaped on political opponents or minorities such as 'the rich'. Taxes would be simple, transparent, easy to pay and predictable. They would not be 'farmed' by public or private agencies that have an interest in boosting the amount they pull in from taxpayers.

The paternalist argument

A very common viewpoint among ruling elites is that they have to take all the decisions because the public are, like children, incapable of making decisions for themselves. This is self-contradictory: it degrades 'the people' from whom their power is supposed to come. And it is illogical to suggest that the people have enough collective wisdom to elect the right government, but not enough individual wisdom to manage their own lives.

There are certainly cases where the whole society would benefit if people behaved a little better. But most of these are moral issues that it is no business of the law to enforce. And while we might *urge* people morally to do things that would help others, the government of a free society cannot *make* them. It is empowered only to prevent harm being done to others, not to force people to benefit others. There is a 'public goods' argument for making people contribute to certain common projects such as defence, but such cases are rare.

It is true that people often show surprising apathy over issues such as how state-run services are delivered. But that is usually

> **Question: Surely we all have responsibilities to the government?**
>
> No. In a free society, the government has responsibilities to us. In many places, governments were established, and remain in power, only through force. This is not a legitimate form of government. The government of a free society is one that is formed by the people as an agency to decide or do those few things that have to be decided or done collectively (such as defence) or impartially (such as justice). It is there to serve the citizens – not the other way round.

because they know that complaining is a waste of breath, since nothing will change. If anything actually improved as a result of people getting involved, more people would.

Ways to limit government
Democracy

In the rare cases where collective decisions are inescapable, a free society consults the whole population, since the whole population is affected by the outcome. In other words, there is some kind of democracy.

It may not be that the whole population takes every decision – that would be far too cumbersome and time-consuming. Normally, the whole population elects representatives to decide on their behalf. Such representatives are not mere delegates, expected slavishly to reflect the views of their electors; they bring their own judgement into the process.

Democracy is not the same as populism. The majority of the

public may well believe that religious or ethnic minorities should be slaughtered, but the government of a free society cannot do that. It exists to *prevent* harm to others, not to facilitate it. An old joke describes democracy as two wolves and a sheep deciding what to have for dinner. But in a free society there are limits on the powers of majorities in order to protect minorities.

The biggest problem is not how to choose governments, but how to restrain them. They are only human: the power they wield can corrupt them. If freedom is to be safeguarded, there must be some mechanism to remove our leaders. Elections in a free society are not just about choosing leaders, but also about getting rid of them.

Some authoritarians argue that elections merely create instability as different governments, perhaps with radically different policies, are voted in and out. But because the power of governments is limited in a free society, the extent of any instability is reduced. If governments are seen to be legitimate, the chances of disruptive instability are smaller, not greater, than if they are not. Through force of arms, an illegitimate government can remain in power a long time; but the only real alternatives are periodic, peaceful elections or occasional, bloody revolutions. In free societies elections are preferred, which limit coercion and violence, and allow change and progress to happen faster.

Certain conditions are required if elections are to be accepted as legitimate. There must, for example, be a genuine choice of parties. It is not a free election if there is only one candidate to vote for: in a free society there will always be a diversity of views. That in turn implies that different candidates must be able to express and publish their views, and be free to criticise other candidates and parties. And people must be able to vote for their preferred candidate without fear of retribution – so ballots must be secret. Some countries put limits on election campaign expenditure in order to ensure that rich candidates or parties do not have an advantage. Many impose fixed terms between elections, rather than allowing the incumbent government to decide when they should be held.

Public decision-making

The governments of most non-free countries came to office through force. Some remain there through force, though many have found ways to give themselves the appearance of legitimacy – by setting themselves up as the sole custodians of the religious or cultural heritage, for example. In a free society, by contrast, government exists only for very limited purposes and by the consent of the public.

Even so, governments often stray well beyond their purposes of preventing harm and doing collectively what cannot be done individually. For example, they often monopolise the delivery of public goods. While decisions about what public goods should be provided might have to be collective, they can still be delivered, in whole or part, by private agencies. Charities, for example, can deliver care to the poor and the sick. And in terms of preventing harm to others – such as the effects of pollution – the degree of harm done can be hard to measure, and government intervention may not in fact be fully justified.

If some decisions must be made collectively, by what rules should those decisions be made? The ideal would be unanimity: everyone takes part in the decision-making, and no action is taken unless everyone agrees. Since people are unlikely to vote for collective action that they think would harm them, there is then little chance of any individuals or groups being harmed by the collective decisions.

But unanimity is hard to achieve. For a start, it would be very time-consuming for every person to take the time to study and vote on every proposal. That is why we elect representatives instead. And reaching any agreement at all would be a struggle, because any one person could veto the whole plan. Hence, collective decisions – whether made through popular elections, referenda or votes in the legislature – are generally made by a majority. It may be a simple (50 per cent +1) majority or a qualified (say two-thirds) majority. That reduces the difficulty of making decisions, while still ensuring that decisions are made by the greater part of the population rather than by small elites.[4]

Voters' self-interest

There is a story about the Roman emperor who, asked to judge the finalists in a singing contest, hears one and gives the prize to the other, on the grounds that the second could not be worse. And today, people have a tendency to think that whenever we are unsatisfied with what a free society and a free economy produce, government action must improve things. If the market fails to deliver public goods such as defence or welfare, for example, the government must provide them instead. Or if a factory pollutes the air, government action is needed to stop it. But this does not necessarily follow.

Markets might indeed fail to meet our needs on occasions.

---

4   For a more detailed summary of this and the following points, see Eamonn Butler, *Public Choice – a Primer*, Institute of Economic Affairs, London, 2012.

But when we speak of 'market failure' we must remember that there is *government failure* too. Even in relatively free societies, governments are not objective, measured, dispassionate, public-spirited forces. Self-interest runs through government, from top to bottom.

People imagine elections as a means to identify the 'public interest' and put it into effect. But in a free society there are many different interests – and those interests conflict. Voters who want lower taxes are at odds with others who want more public spending. Those who would benefit from a new highway oppose those whose homes would be demolished. Elections do not establish 'the' public interest. They simply balance many competing interests. Collective decisions are made on this foundation of conflict.

Politicians' self-interest

Just as voters have their own interests to serve, so do politicians. Many see office as a way to get rich or do down their enemies. They might even be thought weak if they do not exploit office like this. And even in more-free societies, corruption can be a problem.

Even if the politicians really want to serve the public, they first have to get into power. They need to collect enough votes to be elected. But this does not mean that they must therefore reflect broad public opinion. They may win more votes by appealing to small, unrepresentative minorities.

Small groups with strong interests dominate the political process because they have something specific to gain by getting a favourable policy in place – such as a subsidy to their own industry. Being small and highly motivated, they are easy to organise, and more likely to put effort into campaigning and lobbying. But much broader groups, such as consumers or taxpayers, with less specific views, are harder to organise. And they are less motivated, because the costs of policies such as the industry subsidy are spread thinly between them all.

Coalitions and logrolling

The dominance of minority views becomes even greater when interest groups form pacts with others to pool their voting strength. A coalition of several groups, all threatening to desert a candidate, has even more leverage over the candidate than any one alone.

The same pandering to special interests occurs in the legislature. Politicians who desperately want public spending projects in their own district may trade votes with others who desperately want other projects in theirs. But the result of these 'you vote for my measure and I will vote for yours' arrangements – known as *logrolling* – is that more such proposals succeed and that government grows larger than anyone really wants.

And when these laws do go into effect, more self-interest comes into play. The officials who are delegated to administer them will have interests of their own. Their status and pay depend in part on having a large staff, and – consciously or unconsciously – they may make the bureaucratic process more complicated in order to justify that larger staff, a process known as *empire building*. And again, they will receive more lobbying from small interest groups than from the general public, so may concede more to the special interests, and perhaps even take bribes from them.

Setting the rules

To sum up, in choosing governments, making laws and administering laws, minorities with concentrated interests count for more than majorities with more diffused views. Decisions made politically are very poor at reflecting the broad views of the public. And the government sector has an inherent tendency to grow well beyond what most people want, beyond what makes sense and well beyond what is needed to maintain a free society – to the point, indeed, where freedom is actually eroded.

The more-free societies adopt various rules to try to limit these problems. Elections are a vital part of this. But they are a weak restraint on politicians and officials. They come rarely, and are often dominated by larger parties, making change slow. Stronger restraints are needed.

Constitutional agreement

A common way to restrain the political process is to adopt a constitution that is agreed by everyone, or by an overwhelming majority, and which sets out the rules by which elections are run and political decisions are made. If everyone has to agree to what the rules are, it becomes impossible for governments to impose rules designed for their own benefit – for example, by banning opposition candidates or imposing disproportionate taxes on opposition voters.

The political process can be further restrained by the *separation of powers.* Instead of a single person or a single body wielding all the law-making power, the idea is to split that authority between different institutions, each of which can block, modify or restrain what the others can do. For that reason it is sometimes called a system of *checks and balances.*

If a single body, such as a politburo or legislative council, has all the power, political majorities and sectional group interests will certainly try to capture it for their own benefit. But if the constitution divides power between two different chambers of government, it makes power harder for interest groups to capture. If those chambers are elected in different ways, it will be even harder for the same group interests to dominate both. If either chamber can block or modify decisions made in the other, it makes logrolling, and the exploitation of minorities, still more difficult.

As a longstop in this system of checks and balances, many constitutions of more-free societies also appoint a president as the representative of the whole people, who (it is hoped) can rise above the political fray and veto legislation that injures minorities.

A further longstop against exploitation is an *independent judiciary*. This is essential for a free society. Judges must not be politically aligned, and must be able to strike down unconstitutional laws and the exploitation of minorities – and to do so without fear of retribution by politicians.

Constitutions sometimes put other restraints on the activities of government, such as *balanced budgets* – insisting that its budgets should balance over some fixed period (say, three to five years), and setting *budget limits* on annual borrowing and the total of public debt. Some even limit the proportion of the national income that government may spend, in order to curb its inherent tendency to grow. In addition there may be *term limits* so that politicians cannot remain in office for years, and *sunset clauses* to prevent government agencies outliving their usefulness.

Qualified majorities

A further way to protect minorities is through *qualified majority voting*. Freedom would be very insecure, for example, if the ruling authorities were able to change the constitutional rules by a simple vote in the legislature. So a free society sets much higher barriers – such as a two-thirds vote in both chambers plus equally high margins in a plebiscite or in the individual regions or states.

On issues where it is easy to exploit minorities in very damaging ways, decisions should require very high majorities. For example, it is easy to design taxes that can impose very great burdens on particular groups. Some advocates of a free society therefore demand that the tax rules – not the rate of tax but who pays what taxes – must be decided unanimously so that the minority is protected, even if the majority is an overwhelming one.

The captive public

In the market economy, you are free to take your business elsewhere if you feel that a trader is cheating you or giving you poor value for money. But if your government is cheating or exploiting you, there is nowhere else to go. You might perhaps leave the country – but given language and other barriers, this is not an option for most people. This is a recipe for coercion – which makes it all the more important to ensure that the role and actions of government, and every part of it, are carefully specified and strictly limited to those required to preserve and expand the freedom of the population.

4 EQUALITY AND INEQUALITY

Equality in a free society

Many people imagine that free societies must be very unequal. After all, they allow people to pursue and amass great wealth. This (runs the argument) must create great economic inequality.

But this argument is wrong. As we have seen, the disparity in incomes between free and non-free countries is very nearly the same. If anything, the most-free societies are slightly more equal.

Furthermore, non-free societies have other, non-financial inequalities that more-free societies do not. Every citizen of a free society can aspire to increase their wealth and income by moving to a better job, or engaging in commercial activities that will profit them. In non-free societies this is not always possible. Government jobs may be open only to those who support the ruling party, or to friends and associates of the rulers. The law, or prejudice, may bar women, ethnic minorities or other groups from working in certain occupations. People of a particular race or caste may be restricted to the most menial work. Immigrants may be forbidden from setting up and owning businesses, or even holding a bank account.

Even among those who do get work, inequalities persist. In Soviet Moscow, for example, the exclusive GUM department store in Red Square was open only to hard-currency tourists and senior Party officials. Only the latter could aspire to be driven in a Zil limousine – traffic stopped to ease their passage – or enjoy month-long holidays in woodland health spas. Apartments and weekend dachas were allocated by the authorities, who favoured their friends with the better homes.

These are all inequalities from which there is no escape: those who suffer them might not even have the right to vote or campaign for a change in the law. By contrast, all members of a free society can at least aspire to get a good job or set up a business and acquire wealth and income. They may not all succeed, but there is nobody stopping them.

Kinds of equality

Equality in a free society is not about giving people the same wealth or income or standard of living. It is about making sure that people are *treated* the same.

This shows itself in four important ways.[1] The citizens of a free society have *moral equality*: they each have the same right to make choices for themselves and to be treated with consideration and respect by others. There is *equality before the law*: the law protects them and treats them identically, regardless of their race, religion, sex, wealth or family connections. They have *political equality*: they can all vote and stand for political office. And they have *equality of opportunity*: there are no arbitrary barriers to work or schooling or any other route to personal advancement.

---

1   A good outline of these points can be found in Nigel Ashford's *Principles for a Free Society*, Jarl Hjalmarson Foundation, Stockholm, 2003.

Moral equality

In a free society, people are thought equally worthy of consideration and respect. They all have the same right to make choices about their own lives, provided that they do not cause harm to others in the process.

This view is based on a deep belief about their very nature as human beings, the nature which we all share. We all want to make our own choices, regardless of our ethnicity, religion or gender; and we all want others to respect our right to do so. The rule in a free society is 'do as you would be done by'.

This is not to say that people are equally moral in their actions. Those who attack or rob others do not act morally. Some may deliberately flout social or sexual conventions. But their lives remain of value. Their lawbreaking or immorality opens them up to punishment or rebuke that is proportionate to their offence. But it does not open them up to arbitrary or excessive cruelty and humiliation.

Equality before the law

The law in a free society protects and punishes people impartially. Offenders do not receive different treatment by the police, the courts or the prisons because of some personal characteristic that is unrelated to the crime, such as their wealth, connections, caste, gender, religion or ethnicity. Citizens cannot be subjected to arbitrary arrest or harassment just because those in authority dislike them. Everyone has the same access to justice if they are harmed or robbed by others, no matter who they are and no matter how eminent are those they accuse.

In the statuary above the world's court buildings, the figure of justice is usually portrayed as holding a balance in one hand and a sword in the other. But the most important feature is that the figure is blindfolded. In a free society, justice is blind to everything except the relevant facts in each case.

Political equality

Another form of equality that stems from people's nature as human beings is political equality. Everyone's interests and opinions are held worthy of consideration. So everyone in a free society has the right to vote in elections or plebiscites, and nobody has more than one vote. This ensures that everyone's interests are taken into account by candidates and by elected politicians.

There are very limited exceptions. We do not normally allow children to vote, believing they are not yet mature enough to express a considered opinion on how they and others should be governed. Similarly, people with severe mental disabilities may also be excluded from voting; but such incapacity must be assessed independently in order to prevent the ruling elites excluding their opponents on these grounds.

Opinions are divided on whether convicted criminals should be allowed to vote. In some countries, people in jail lose their right to vote, on the grounds that someone who has seriously broken the laws should not be involved in the process of making them. In others, only those imprisoned for the most serious offences are excluded. In yet others, criminals are seen as fully entitled to vote by virtue of the nature we all share as human beings.

The principle of political equality means that women are as entitled to vote as men are – though, even in relatively free societies, this right has been recognised for little more than a century.

New Zealand was the first, granting adult women the right to vote in 1893. Australia did the same in 1902, though restrictions on voting by Aboriginal women persisted until 1962. Most European countries allowed women votes soon after World War I, though in France it was as late as 1944, and in Switzerland 1971.

Any exceptions to the right to vote should be strictly limited. It is too easy for the authorities in non-free countries to deny their enemies the vote by dispatching them to jail or declaring them mentally incapable or a large variety of other excuses. That is an abuse of power.

As far as practicable, each person's vote should also count equally. For example, there should be roughly equal numbers of electors in each electoral district from which representatives are chosen. Larger districts mean that each voter has less say in the result. The only excuse for having districts with very different sizes is the brute realities of geography. Electoral boundaries must be decided by independent bodies so that they cannot be skewed to benefit ruling groups.

Along with the right to vote, everyone has an equal right to stand for and hold office. There are no seats in the legislature that are restricted to people of a particular gender, race or religion. The electoral system must safeguard this equality, ensuring, for example, that anyone can stand for office without fear of being threatened or intimidated – particularly by the ruling political authorities. That means that they must be free to campaign and to speak, publish and broadcast their views and their criticisms of other candidates and indeed of the laws and the constitution. Elections are supposed to be a contest of ideas, and there can be no free elections if ideas and free speech are suppressed. In some non-free countries it is a criminal offence to criticise the government; in the more-free societies, such criticism is a perfectly normal part of everyday political debate.

Equality of opportunity

Equality of opportunity means that individuals should not face arbitrary barriers to pursuing their own ambitions, in education, work, or any other part of life. Their race should not bar them from a place in school or in a sports team, for example. Their politics or their gender should not deny them the chance of a job. Nor should their poverty or social class prevent them from marrying someone from different circumstances.

This does not mean, however, that schools or employers or anyone else are forced to take in anyone, regardless of their qualifications. A school may well restrict its admissions to those who pass an examination, and an employer may demand references and experience. A free woman does not have to marry a man just because he has set his heart on her. Equality of opportunity means only that there are no arbitrary obstacles put in anyone's way, and that they are not coerced into doing something they do not want to do. For example, arranged marriages are common in some cultures and are perfectly acceptable in a free society provided that both partners consent. But people cannot be *forced* to marry against their wishes, even if their parents demand it. In a free society, someone old enough to marry is considered old enough to choose for themselves. Like any other contract, a marriage is void if either partner is coerced into it.

Though people should face no social barriers in their life choices, there are of course natural inequalities. Someone born deaf is unlikely to become a composer or an orchestra conductor

Question: Poor people are not free to buy limousines, are they?

Yes, they are. In a free society, everyone is *free* to buy luxury goods, even if only a few can *afford* them. It is a question of power, not freedom; poorer people lack the *purchasing power* to buy a big car; but no person or authority prevents them. Anyone can aspire to own luxuries, by working hard to earn money, by saving or even borrowing.

Remember also that even poorer families in the world's wealthiest and most-free societies now enjoy things such as domestic heat, light, power and running water that were luxuries only a few decades ago. In non-free societies, by contrast, people cannot even aspire to things such as a bigger house or a more fertile farm plot unless the authorities grant them these things.

(though in later life, Beethoven managed it). A limbless person cannot aspire to climb mountains. And children get different starts in life depending on their family circumstances: the parents of one might buy them books and help them with schoolwork, while the parents of another might neglect them.

Some people in the West argue that, even though children get different starts in life, schools should aim to ensure that they reach the same position by the time they reach adulthood and enter the workforce. Accordingly, schools focus huge resources on remedial education, and 'level down' the brightest children rather than stretching them to their full potential. But in reality, we cannot compensate for natural differences – and the only way of compensating for social differences would be the nightmare prospect of the state taking children from their parents at birth and raising them identically.

Positive discrimination

Some countries have attempted to compensate for natural differences, and to break down prejudice, with programmes of positive discrimination. This may involve simply reaching out to minorities who may not imagine that certain opportunities are within their grasp – bright but poor children, for example, who may never think of applying for a top university – and encouraging them to try. Such outreach and encouragement are unobjectionable, since they simply increase the options available to these groups.

But positive discrimination may also take the form of giving preference to minority groups – say, imposing quotas on schools and employers in order to force them to take a larger proportion of minority candidates. Up to a point, this may work: arguably, positive discrimination in the United States from the 1960s onwards allowed blacks to show their capabilities in schools and workplaces, and so helped break down white prejudice against them. But positive discrimination is not compatible with a free society. While it may help to break down prejudice and therefore promote freedom, it favours particular groups instead of treating them equally.

Some people argue for preferences and quotas on the grounds of making up for past negative discrimination against minorities. But bygones are bygones: discriminating positively in favour of some people today does not rectify the injustice done to others from the same minority who were harmed in the past. And such a policy may well be seen as unfair to the majority, who must reach higher standards in order to have the same school or job opportunities. The minority may come to be seen as the new privileged class, and there may be a backlash of resentment or even violence against the policy and the minorities that benefit from it.

Negative discrimination

Discrimination is not always intended to help minorities, of course. Much more often, discrimination is a case of the majority voting themselves rights, privileges and preferences that are not available to minority groups. Malaysia and South Africa are two obvious examples, but the world abounds with cases in which the law discriminates against minority populations solely on the grounds of their race, religion, language, sexual preferences or political views.

Again, such discrimination has no place in a free society: in a free society, people are equal before the law and no group can vote itself special privileges. Too often, this sort of discrimination has drifted into becoming outright persecution of the minority populations. Stripped of the rights enjoyed by the majority, the minority have no way to improve themselves. They can become seen as an underclass, even as subhuman. And when their humanity is stripped away, there is no limit to the indignity and maltreatment they might suffer.

Equality of outcome

When most people talk about equality, they do not mean the right to equal treatment under the principles of moral equality, equality before the law, political equality and equality of opportunity. They mean equality in *material rewards* such as wealth, income and living standards. And many advocate some form of *redistribution* from rich to poor in order to equalise these rewards.

Income inequality statistics

People who advocate equality of outcome often cite a statistic called the *Gini coefficient*, named after the Italian statistician and sociologist Corrado Gini. It is an index of inequality in measures such as income. A Gini coefficient of 0 means that there is complete equality, a coefficient of 1 means complete inequality (as when one person has all the income).

Various institutions such as the World Bank and the US Central Intelligence Agency attempt to measure the Gini coefficients of different countries and thus rank them in terms of their inequality. Such rankings suggest that most of the advanced countries have coefficients ranging from 0.25 to around 0.5 – meaning a high level of equality. The greatest inequality is shown in African countries, topped by South Africa with a coefficient of around 0.7.

We should remain sceptical about such calculations, and even more so about the suggestion that incomes in high-coefficient countries should be forcibly equalised. In the first place, few countries have reliable data on incomes, making the Gini coefficient an equally unreliable measure (which may be why the different institutions that calculate it come up with different figures). Secondly, large income differences may reflect social trends that are actually positive. They might indicate rapid growth in new technologies, or rising prosperity in the cities, which has not yet reached the countryside. It would make no sense to choke off this rising prosperity by reducing the incomes of city IT workers to those of subsistence farmers. Rather, we should make it feasible for poorer people to share in this prosperity by removing the barriers (such as restrictions on free movement) that currently prevent them doing so.

Another problem with the statistics is that they compare 'raw' incomes, ignoring the taxes people pay and the government benefits (welfare, pensions, free healthcare and so on) they receive. To take a slightly different sort of measure from the United Kingdom, the raw incomes of the top 10 per cent of earners are about 30 times those of the bottom 10 per cent, which looks like huge inequality. Yet after people have paid their taxes and received their various government benefits the multiple is a much more modest 6. People still cite the first figure in order to justify further redistribution, but this is a fraudulent use of statistics.

Equality of income or wealth?

The idea that people should enjoy equal rewards from their participation in society is called *egalitarianism*. But it can be hard to pin down the exact meaning of this term, partly because of its own contradictions.

Egalitarians can be vague about whether they want equality of incomes – or of wealth. If they mean that *incomes* should be equal, they would have to accept that large differences in wealth would almost certainly still occur. One person might save and invest their income wisely and accrue capital and wealth, while another on the same income might gamble it away or spend it on instant gratification. Before long, their wealth would be very different.

Also, if all jobs paid equally, there would be a massive

over-demand for jobs that were easy and pleasant and a massive shortage of people willing to do jobs that were difficult and unpleasant. Why should anyone bother to work hard if they are rewarded identically to their lazy colleagues?

There is also more to a job than material income. There is what economists call *psychological income* – having agreeable workmates, for example, or working in a nice part of the country or a convenient and well-provided part of a city. These qualities may be worth a great deal to those who enjoy them, but they are not things that can be equalised.

If, on the other hand, egalitarians mean that *wealth* should be equalised, there could still be large differences in incomes, depending on people's skills and talents and on employers' demand for them. And if some people saved and added to their wealth, while others spent and reduced it, their fortunes would soon diverge. What to do then? Wilfred Pickles, the host of a popular 1950s UK radio quiz show, *Have a Go*, would start by asking contestants about themselves and their ambitions. One said: 'My ambition is to get all the money in the world and divide it equally between everyone.' There was loud applause at this charitable sentiment. Unfortunately the contestant spoiled the effect by adding: 'And when I had spent my share we would do it again.' In a changing world it is hard to keep wealth equal.

Equal outcomes, either of income or wealth, are therefore both unnatural and unstable. To equalise either, and keep them equalised, would require a massive assault on liberty and property. It would involve taking wealth by force from some people and giving it to others – and doing so over and over again in order to keep things anywhere near equal.

Some wealth is impossible to break up and redistribute: a

complex, functioning, wealth-producing factory might be broken into its component bricks and machine parts, but would then produce nothing. Nor could it be sold off in order to redistribute the money – in a world of equal wealth, no individual would have the resources to buy it.

Such redistribution policies would be coercive and highly inefficient. They would deny people the fruits of their own labour and erode all incentives to work and save. They would destroy wealth rather than just redistribute it. And they would require huge political power to enforce – power that is incompatible with a free society.

The mechanics of redistribution

Another problem is deciding who exactly should be part of the redistribution process. Usually, egalitarians in wealthy countries confine their proposals to residents of their own country, or at most a group of similar countries. That is because to share income or wealth equally with the rest of the world would mean (even if it were practicable) a huge drop in living standards for people in the rich countries. It is not a policy that is likely to be accepted peacefully.

Egalitarians in poor countries, by contrast, generally have a world vision of equality: sharing out the wealth of the rich countries, they reason, would make a huge difference to their impoverished populations. But that is an impossible dream, since the richer countries would never agree.

Nor would such redistribution actually secure lasting wealth for the poor. Wealth is not a 'zero-sum game'. There is no fixed pool of wealth such that one person can become richer only if another is made poorer. Wealth is *created* through innovation, enterprise, trade and building capital. Destroying the productive capital of those who have it does nothing to help those who do not. A better policy is to tackle the disincentives, such as war and theft, which discourage people in poorer nations from accumulating capital of their own.

These questions about what would be redistributed, and to and from whom, make it plain that there can never be any agreement on what a redistribution policy would look like. Yet to make redistribution work, there has to be a definite plan, to which everyone conforms. In the absence of agreement, the only way to achieve that is by force.

Forced submission to material equality would completely kill the point of anyone striving for something better. Since any material benefit you achieved through innovation, enterprise or hard work would be taken away, why should anyone strive to achieve? And there is an even more profound loss to humanity than this. Enterprise is creative: people striving to produce better goods and services hit on new products, processes and technologies that improve the lives of everyone. By stifling that enterprise and creativity, egalitarianism closes off the prospect of continual improvement in the material lives of the whole world.

Equality and justice
Two meanings of justice

Many people who favour the redistribution of wealth or incomes argue that it is 'unjust' that some people are richer than others – and that a few may be far richer than the very poorest. This 'social injustice' is compounded by the fact that people's wealth does not necessarily reflect their 'value to society'.

This argument hijacks the word 'justice', however – which we all accept is a good and desirable thing, and something due to each of us as human beings – and gives it a completely different meaning, that of equality or fairness.

The original meaning of justice concerns what conduct we expect from each other. If someone breaches a contract or steals, we say they have acted unjustly, because such behaviour is forbidden under the no-harm principle and under our legal and moral rules. In other words, this meaning of justice, called *commutative justice*, is about how human beings behave. It applies only where people act deliberately. If someone contracts influenza or suffers a physical disability, it is a misfortune, but it is not unjust, because nobody has acted unjustly.

The second use of the word 'justice', sometimes called *distributive justice*, is not about the conduct between individuals, but about the distribution of things between them. Yet in a free society, the distribution of wealth or income that emerges is simply the *outcome* of voluntary economic activity where everyone follows the legal and moral rules. It cannot be 'unjust' because nobody has acted unjustly. Nobody intended this particular outcome; it is just a fact of life.[2]

'Value to society'

The use of the term 'social justice' makes the mistake that society is a sort of person who decides the pattern of wealth and income. But 'society' has no will of its own: only individuals can make decisions and act upon them. And individuals disagree strongly on

---

2   This and the following points are well made in F. A. Hayek, *The Mirage of Social Justice*, University of Chicago Press, Chicago, IL, 1978.

matters of social and economic policy. One reason why the idea of 'social justice' appeals to so many people is that it is extremely vague about what the exact outcome should be, and glosses over these disagreements.

When we try to flesh out what a 'socially just' distribution of rewards might look like, the impossibility of reaching agreement about it becomes obvious. Most people agree that *complete equality of incomes* is not the right target, because then individuals would get the same rewards no matter how lazy or obstructive they chose to be. Plainly, reward must take effort or achievement into account. A common view, therefore, is that instead of complete equality, rewards should be allocated according to people's 'value to society'.

But then who is to decide a person's 'value to society'? Society is not a person, and has no values of its own. People cannot attribute 'value' to something that has no values of its own. Only *individuals* have values, and those values are widely different and indeed often conflict. One group of people might value the performance of a boxer, while others might appreciate that of a violin player; it is impossible to say which delivers the greater 'value to society' because the enjoyment of different people cannot be compared. How could we ever decide the 'value to society' of a nurse, a butcher, a coal miner, a judge, a deep-sea diver, a tax inspector, the inventor of a life-saving drug or a professor of mathematics?

Distribution on merit

Another suggestion from egalitarians is that rewards should be distributed on 'merit'. But again, there is no dispassionate way of deciding the relative 'merit' of different people and how it should be rewarded. Different people might take very different views on how commendable different qualities happen to be.

Even then there are practical issues in deciding how much merit is involved. Should the 'merit' of someone who invests years of toil but fails be rewarded, while someone who brings value to millions be penalised because it was the result of a lucky accident? We do not want to encourage fruitless toil: economic progress is about raising the value of what we produce and reducing the sacrifice that goes into it. Rewarding people for personal sacrifice would simply encourage sacrifice, not service to others. No economy could run on such a principle.

Market rewards do not reflect the moral and personal merits of producers, nor the time and effort they spend in bringing their goods and services to market. It does not matter whether their products required years of toil and investment or were the result of a lucky accident. But market rewards do reflect the enjoyment and value that people deliver to others. Customers pay producers for the goods and services they produce because they value those products. And in that very real sense, market rewards do depend on the value that people deliver to other members of society. They also reflect the scarcity and talent of the producers, the numbers of customers who want the service and the urgency or importance that buyers attach to having it.

Distribution according to need

Another egalitarian suggestion is that resources should be distributed according to 'need'. But again, who is to decide what 'need' is? There is no obvious line that separates needy from non-needy people. People's circumstances are very varied; they have different wealth and income, but this may fluctuate greatly. They also live in nicer or nastier places, have different physical and mental abilities, and work with different people in different jobs. These nonfinancial benefits such as having an agreeable job with friendly work colleagues are impossible to put figures on.

Whether people are 'needy' or not, therefore, is a matter of judgement, and different people would assess it differently. Redistribution on the basis of need would be feasible only if some political authority was given the power to decide 'need' and act upon it. But people in a free society could never agree to give such power to any authority. It would be complete power over their lives. They would no longer be free people. They would be slaves to that authority.

Nor does the existence of need create an *obligation* on others. A person with kidney failure might be in need of a new kidney. But that does not oblige anyone else to donate one of their own. Close relatives may feel a moral and family duty to donate, and even strangers may be moved by compassion. But it remains their choice. We might encourage and applaud such actions, but a free society cannot *compel* individuals to make sacrifices in order to help others.

A free economy distributes things, not through any compulsion, but through the values that purchasers put on the different goods and services that a market economy produces. If people prefer organic to farmed fish, for example, or shoes to sandals, then that is what is produced. And it distributes resources too through the values that people express in their philanthropic gifts to others. Such decisions are left to individuals: the idea that only the state can know what causes deserve support is rejected in a free society.

Further damage of egalitarianism

A damaging result of the egalitarian focus on 'social justice' is that it eclipses the idea and the reality of genuine, commutative justice. The basic principles that make a free society – such as equality before the law – are obscured and devalued by this new term. With redistribution, there can be no equality of treatment: instead of treating people all the same, we would have to take differing amounts from each contributor and give differing amounts to each recipient.

Material desires persist

While real justice exists to settle conflicts, 'social justice' actually creates them. Once a government tries to redistribute income on the basis of merit, or need, or value to society, it will find itself being lobbied by many different groups, all claiming that their rewards should be increased. Since there is no real way to decide between them, this political conflict will prompt arbitrary decisions. Brute power ultimately decides things, which is incompatible with a free society.

And individuals will try to find ways round the system in order to benefit themselves and their families. This was certainly the experience in the Soviet Union, where probably the majority of the population were engaged in some kind of illicit activity to improve their standard of living. Forced material equality simply turns otherwise law-abiding people into a nation of criminals.

Role of the rich

Inequalities of income and wealth also have positive functions.

The desire of people to earn more and maybe become rich is a powerful incentive. It stimulates them to seek out better jobs, and to invent, produce and distribute better products that improve the lives of other people. Rich people have an important role as test drivers of these new goods.

Most new products come on to the market as luxuries – without having established a mass market, they are made in small quantities, at high cost. So they are bought and tried out by wealthier people. Those people's feedback enables producers to establish the level of demand for the product and where and how it needs improvement. It allows them to abandon faulty products before committing to large production runs, and to improve the quality of the products that do come on to the mass market. In this way, the experience of rich, pioneering customers benefits everyone.

People with wealth and high incomes have other important social roles. They have the resources to experiment in providing new products and services, which expands choice and feeds the process of improvement. They can sponsor the arts, education and research projects that they believe the government is neglecting. And they have the financial backing to challenge an oppressive authority by propagating new political ideas that government officials might see as deeply threatening. These are all important considerations if we are to preserve a free society.

The destruction of capital

Not everyone is equally good at managing productive resources. Those who make a career as entrepreneurs have to be: if they are to make profit from their ventures, they need to know how to manage risks and bring together productive resources in order to produce better and cheaper goods. But redistribution would take resources out of the hands of these skilled practitioners, and spread them around to others. That means a loss of capital and of capital creation. But capital is what makes an economy productive; with less being created, and more resources simply being consumed, the long-term prosperity of society must inevitably decline.

Inequality too drives economic improvement. The high gains made by successful producers act as a magnet, pulling people and resources to where the greatest value can be gained, and away from less productive and valuable uses. So people and resources are attracted to where they will add most to future incomes. It is a continuous, dynamic, growing process. The inequality that so many people resent is, in fact, the very attraction that steers people and resources to their most productive uses, raising prosperity everywhere. If we redistribute incomes in pursuit of equality, we block that attractive force, and lose the future value, output and growth that it could generate. With so many poor people depending on a rising economy, it is they who would suffer most. How can we call that 'social justice'?

Taxation and welfare

Complete equality of wealth or incomes might be an impossible objective, but many governments nevertheless try to get near it, with progressive taxes that impose higher rates of tax on richer people. But these taxes can be highly damaging. By reducing the rewards from enterprise and effort, they discourage these useful activities – and the employment and improvement they create.

Worse still, such taxes are often levied on savings and capital. Taxes on savings leave people with less money to invest in business ventures that raise the prosperity of the whole society. Taxes on capital mean that fewer resources will go into building up productive assets, reducing the future prosperity of the whole community.

In a free society, commerce and exchange are purely voluntary. Producers make money only by creating products and services that other people want and are prepared to pay for. People who become rich rob nobody. They are not guilty of any injustice. We would not allow a robber to steal from them on the grounds that this would reduce material inequality: so why should we allow governments to do it?

5 FREE ENTERPRISE AND TRADE

The free-market economy

The economic system in a free society is the free-market economy. It works through the voluntary exchange of goods and services between people – sometimes directly but usually through the medium of money. Individuals are free to choose if, how, when, where and with whom they work, spend, invest, save and trade. Nobody is forced into such transactions.

Rules to promote cooperation

The free-market economy is not a lawless free-for-all in which people can do what they want, regardless of the consequences for others. The no-harm principle still prevails. And there is a framework of law, which covers the acquisition, ownership and exchange of property, people's rights over their own labour, and the enforceability of contracts. These rules cover not just the behaviour of individuals, but groups such as partnerships, companies and charities. The role of government is to maintain the rules that protect people's property and freedom, and to enforce their contracts.

That role is limited, however. The rules are not there to direct commerce, but to facilitate it. They are like a fire basket that contains the fire. And it is important that the energy of the market economy is not smothered by excessive rules and regulations. But the basic rules of property, exchange and contract allow people to cooperate, however they choose, for mutual benefit, on a basis of trust, confidence and security. That encourages greater economic cooperation and multiplies the many benefits that stem from it.

The benefits of voluntary exchange

It is easy to imagine that only sellers benefit from commerce. After all, they end with more money from the deal, while the buyer ends up with less. That makes some people think that sellers are greedy and interested in their own profit, not in other people.

This is mistaken. What, after all, is the point of money? In the days when money comprised gold and silver, it at least had some use as a metal that could be made into jewellery and ornaments. But money made from paper and base metals has few other uses. The only useful thing you can do with it is to exchange it for other goods and services.

In other words, money is a *medium of exchange*. A buyer exchanges it for a good or service; the seller then exchanges it for different goods and services from someone else. Both consider themselves better off from the deal. They would not agree to it otherwise.

How trade creates value

Since nobody would exchange one thing for another that is worth less, how can both end up better off? The reason is that value, like beauty, is in the eye of the beholder. It is not some scientific quality of objects, like weight or size. It is what each individual thinks of that object. People in a rainy country would put little value on a cup of water; but those in the desert might consider it precious. A new clothing fashion may be a must-have for teenagers, while their parents might think it ridiculous.

It is precisely because human beings differ in how they value things that they can each gain from exchange. A customer buying a chicken from a market trader values the chicken more than the money exchanged for it. But the trader values the money more than the chicken. When the trader then uses the money to buy other things – bread, say – the same happens. The trader values the bread more than the money that the baker demands for it. All three have gained, which is why they all voluntarily agree to these exchanges.

In fact, the *greater* the difference in value that they put on the chicken, the money and the bread, the more they each gain from exchanging them. All they need to agree on is the rules by which they trade things – the rules of property, honesty and contract that form the framework of the free-market economy. Apart from that, the partners in each deal are entirely self-interested: each makes their exchanges to benefit themselves, not to benefit the other person.

Yet by following these rules, each unintentionally benefits the others – as if guided by 'an invisible hand', as Adam Smith put it.[1] Though motivated only by self-interest, they willingly cooperate with each other.

Through the medium of money, each of us can now trade – and cooperate – not just with others in the same marketplace but with millions of others in countries we will never visit, whose

---

[1]   Adam Smith, *The Wealth of Nations*, 1776, Book IV, ch. II, para. IX.

languages we cannot speak and whose cultures and politics we may even disapprove of. In these countless daily transactions, each side gains. People cooperate. Value is created. Human beings are made better off. Humanity prospers.

The poor gain most

So natural and beneficial is this free exchange system that it has spread everywhere. It even exists illicitly, or is tolerated, in countries that reject free markets as a matter of ideology. Many countries (including several in Asia) that grant their citizens little freedom in personal and social matters nevertheless allow them considerable economic freedom.

Indeed, commerce and trade were important factors in the early years of the Islamic world and its subsequent spread. The opening up of world trade routes created the enormous wealth of Renaissance Europe, which in turn produced a flowering of art, culture and learning. The Americas prospered through their trading links with Europe, and then China.

But it is not the rich who are buoyed up most by this rising tide of human prosperity. Where economic freedom has spread, the living standards of the poor have risen the most. As the American economist Milton Friedman put it, domestic running water was an unimaginable luxury in Imperial Rome; but a Roman senator had no need of it because he had running servants to bring it instead.[2] The poor of Imperial Rome lived in squalor; but the poor of modern Rome now take the luxury of hot and cold running water for granted.

---

2   Milton Friedman and Rose Friedman, *Free to Choose*, Harcourt Brace Jovanovich, New York, 1980, p. 147.

This effect can be seen vividly in the recent opening up of international trade and the spread of market principles in countries such as China and India. In just three decades, perhaps a billion or more people have been raised out of abject poverty as a result. Millions more can now aspire to be middle class and to enjoy luxuries such as mobile phones, televisions and motor transport – and indeed to work in cool, dry, comfortable offices and factories rather than out in all weathers on the land.

How to grow rich
Producers have to serve customers

In a free society, customers have choice. They are not forced to buy from particular producers, such as the monopolies run by governments or their cronies. Providers may try to collude to raise prices, but it is hard to make such collusion stick, since any of them could cheat by lowering their prices to attract more customers. Meanwhile, other providers are free to enter the market and compete with the firms that are trying to keep prices high.

In a genuinely competitive free-market economy, therefore, producers have no power to exploit their customers. Unless they produce what customers want, with the quality they want and at a price that is attractive, they will soon lose business. Individuals are not held prisoner to the power of corporations. On the contrary, producers survive only by responding to the changing demands of the public.

A company may be big, but it still faces competition. A large firm probably makes many different products and is engaged in many different businesses. But not only does it face potential competition from other big companies. It also faces competition from many smaller ones that can compete for particular parts of the business. Smaller companies with fewer overheads may be able to produce some of the large company's products better or more cheaply. New and innovative companies may produce new products that render one or more of the large company's products obsolete.

It is a myth, therefore, that capitalism leads to bigger and bigger companies, and eventually to monopolies, as firms pursue economies of scale. Scale has its costs too: large organisations are very difficult to manage and slow on their feet. It is instructive to look at any Western magazine of, say, fifty years ago. Few of the companies then advertising still exist. They have all been overtaken by competitors who started small but were more innovative or cost-effective.

No hold on economic power

So, there is no intergenerational hold on economic power by companies, nor by the people who run them. Individuals can become wealthy in a free economy, but only so long as they continue to serve the public and attract customers. Indeed, 'from shirt sleeves to shirt sleeves in three generations' is a common phenomenon in the more-free societies: people set up companies and make money for their families, but by the time their grandchildren come into the business, other companies have begun to outcompete them.

This is a much fairer system than where elites control access to both political and economic power, and make sure that they and their families hold on to it. In a free economy, anyone with talent and determination can aspire to build wealth – provided that they serve others. The chance of becoming wealthy is not restricted to the friends, family or party of those in power, nor to those in

Question: Aren't competition, profit and advertising wasteful?

No. Profit is what spurs people to perform, to search out opportunities and to create the products and services that other people quite willingly choose to buy. Profit also indicates that resources are being used to produce goods or services that the community values more than the raw resources themselves.

Advertising is important because it tells people about new products and improvements to existing products. Competition gives people a choice between different products, pushing suppliers to innovate and provide better quality at lower cost. Without competition, consumers would be powerless. They would have to take what the monopoly provider deigned to supply – or go without.

particular ethnic or religious groups. Indeed, some of the most prosperous people in free societies are immigrants, who come in with different experiences and ideas and produce new products or services that people are keen to buy.

Where there is a powerful government that can dispense favours to its friends, however, business people will try to use it for their own benefit. They may seek regulation that keeps out competitors, or even a complete monopoly. Though they might try to justify this by saying that it will protect the public from substandard goods, their real motive is to corner the market. But this would give them a coercive power that is incompatible with a free society. Governments should not have the power to skew markets and create monopolies; rather, their role should be to extend freedom and competition.

Entrepreneurship

Success in a free economy is not always about working hard – though that often helps. You have to supply goods and services that other people want and are willing to buy. That can involve taking a risk – guessing what new products people will demand – and organising a chain of production that may involve many other suppliers, workers and distributors. Comparatively few people are willing to take on these risks and responsibilities; but the successful anticipation of demand and organisation of production systems, networks and effort is the real contribution of these *entrepreneurs*. They take big risks, and if the public do indeed buy their products, they are well rewarded.

That in turn encourages productivity and innovation. It spurs people into creating new and better products and processes in the hope that they too will achieve the wealth that past entrepreneurs have acquired. And that constant improvement and invention benefits customers and therefore benefits the whole society. Inventions that save people labour or otherwise improve their lives raise prosperity and spread wealth far better than any government welfare scheme.

Customers benefit from goods and services they could never find or produce on their own. It takes a good deal of research and expertise, for example, to develop and supply an effective medicine. Individuals are unlikely to have the chemical, biological and manufacturing expertise needed – but specialist drugs firms do. Even local pharmacists can accrue specialist knowledge of the use, efficacy and side effects of perhaps five hundred or more medicines in their stock. Customers could not possibly acquire such specialist knowledge – certainly not if they also had to become experts on food, drink, clothes, shoes and all the other things that they need in their daily lives.

Entrepreneurs may accumulate wealth. But they do not do it at other people's expense. The money they earn comes only from the voluntary payments of their customers. They get rich only by helping others, not by taxing or exploiting people. And they keep their wealth only as long as they continue to serve the public. To keep earning, they have to understand their customers and anticipate their needs. So they are always looking for some unfilled product niche and seeking to fill it. It is a constant process of trying to keep customers satisfied.

Profit and speculation

The prospect of profit, then, spurs producers – big and small – to take risks, innovate, organise and work to serve other people.

Many critics of free economies disparage the idea of 'profit' – but actually all of us are profit seekers. We sacrifice some things in order to gain something that we value more. For example, we spend time and effort cleaning in order to have a neat and tidy house. We value the clean house more than the effort of cleaning: the difference is our profit. It is not a financial profit, but in other ways it is just like an entrepreneur buying in supplies and producing something that sells for more than the inputs cost. Even when we engage in community or philanthropic projects – serving on a school board, say – we do it for our own ends, even though these ends may be that we want to see all local children well educated. That too is a (non-financial) profit to us. But it is only *financial* profit which critics seem to notice and dislike. This is illogical and inconsistent.

The same is true when *speculation* is criticised. In reality, speculation is not confined to financial markets. We are all speculators. Farmers plant seeds in the hope of raising a marketable crop. We go to school to gain qualifications that we hope will make us more employable. These are speculative ventures.

In the financial world, speculation is hugely important. Ships would never sail if insurance companies and underwriters were not prepared to speculate and take a risk on their safe passage. Much modern production relies on large and long-term contracts – such as supply agreements, or contracts to build and maintain a factory. Individual producers cannot reasonably take on the whole risk. So they invite others to buy shares in their enterprise. That is another form of speculation. In stock markets, speculators buy and sell in the hope of making profits, but to do so they need to have an expert understanding of the firms they are trading, and of their future prospects. That expertise brings useful information to the market, and helps prices reach their right level more quickly than they would without it, making the whole market more responsive and efficient.

Making a profit is not the same as being greedy. People pursue profit for their own self-interest, but that is not the same as greed. Some measure of self-interest is essential if we are each to survive, avoid injury and nourish our bodies. But greed is a moral notion, indicating that someone is excessively self-interested, to the detriment of others. In a free society, producers can satisfy their self-interest only by helping others.

Business and relationships

Crucial though it is, business is not the whole of life. Even the most hard-working business person in a free society has family and other interests such as sports or hobbies, or groups and associations with shared enthusiasms. One need only look at capitalist countries such as Italy, where family relationships are very strong, to realise that family and the market economy sit easily together.

Being in business does not justify treating other people callously, and certainly does not justify harming others – that is ruled out by the no-harm principle. And many of the most rewarding relationships are actually with business colleagues in the workplace. A free-market economy promotes social relationships in other ways too. It gives people the wealth and time to devote to other interests, such as religious or community organisations and philanthropic causes.

How markets work
The telecommunications system of prices

Most markets work through the medium of money. There can be direct exchange – bartering or swapping – without it; but money brings convenience. A seller can exchange a good or service for it, then shop around for the best value before exchanging it for other goods and services. It means that hungry barbers do not need to seek out bakers who need haircuts in order to trade.

Prices are usually expressed in money. Prices are not a standard of value, because value exists in the minds of those involved and different people value the same thing differently. But prices reveal something about people's demand for products and about their scarcity. They reflect the rate at which people are prepared to exchange one thing for another.

As an indicator of scarcity, prices are hard to beat.[3] And not

---

3   These points are made well in F. A. Hayek, *Individualism and Economic Order*, University of Chicago Press, Chicago, IL, 1949. For a brief summary, see Eamonn

only do they reveal where demand is strong. High prices also induce suppliers to meet that demand. Seeing the high prices, producers step into the market in order to capture the potential profit, focusing resources such as labour and capital on satisfying the demand. Low prices, similarly, indicate that demand is weak and that resources are better used elsewhere.

In this way, prices play a vital role in a free economy, helping move resources to where the need for them is highest and drawing them away from where there are surpluses. They also help squeeze out waste: to make the highest profit, suppliers need to find the most cost-effective inputs. That helps conserve resources and ensure that they are used as productively as they can be.

This effect spreads out from market to market across the whole economy, and indeed across the whole world. For example, suppose that some new use is discovered for tin. Manufacturers then start demanding more tin. They will be prepared to pay more for it than before. The high prices will induce mining companies to produce more tin, and wholesalers to supply it. But equally, other users of tin will start looking for substitutes, rather than pay the higher prices. They will demand more of those substitutes, and their price will rise. That encourages people to produce more of the substitutes, and induces users to look for substitutes for those substitutes.

In this way, prices transmit information about scarcity throughout the entire economic system. The Nobel economist F. A. Hayek called it the 'vast telecommunications system' of the market, constantly revealing where surpluses and shortages exist and telling people where best to commit their effort and resources.

Butler, *Friedrich Hayek: The Ideas and Influence of the Libertarian Economist*, Harriman House, Petersfield, 2012.

Markets cannot be perfect

If you read an economics textbook, you might get the impression that markets rely on 'perfect competition' between large numbers of identical suppliers selling identical products to identical customers. They do not. These are only theoretical abstractions. In reality, markets work – and can only work – because people and products are *different*.

If everyone shared the same values, nobody would ever trade anything. Both sides would value goods identically, so there would be no point in exchanging them. Exchange happens only because we disagree on value. And again, if each supplier offered identical products at identical prices, there would be nothing for customers to choose between them. No supplier could beat the competition and earn high profits.

But higher profits are what drive entrepreneurs to outdo the competition. They do that by making their product cheaper – say, by streamlining production. But more importantly, they do it by making their own particular product better. They innovate and differentiate their products. They give consumers something new and better than the old goods they are used to. And they highlight those changes in the hope that buyers will indeed prefer their products to those of others.

This makes free markets amazingly dynamic – not static, frozen and unmoving like the textbook supply and demand graphs. Suppliers are constantly innovating to produce more attractive products, and customers are constantly looking out for improvements.

The impossibility of central planning

Government attempts to steer the economy and produce the goods that people want cannot match the dynamism of this market system.

There are few pressures on government monopolies to innovate. Nor can government bureaucrats know what members of the public actually want and value. They might undertake occasional opinion polls, but that is far removed from the constant competition of the market, in which consumers' buying choices give producers minute-by-minute information about their demand.

To succeed, entrepreneurs have to understand their customers. They cannot wait years to get their opinion on a whole package of products, as governments do at elections. They need to keep alert to what customers want, and on the cost and availability of supplies and inputs. An estate agent, for example, needs to know what is happening in the local property market – which potential buyers are interested in certain types of houses, for example – not just from month to month, but from day to day and even from hour to hour. No central authority could even collect this rapidly changing information, never mind act on it before it all changes again.

Some people think that because a free economy is not planned from the centre, it must be haphazard and irrational. In fact, markets are very orderly. By following the agreed rules of property and exchange, people are able to trade and cooperate, and anticipate the actions of others, with great certainty. Markets are more rational too. They use the local expertise and knowledge of millions of individuals, who are all making their own plans and adjusting to the changing plans of others. A lot more planning

Question: Haven't free markets failed to protect the environment?

No. Markets have not failed. There is simply no market in many environmental goods. Markets work well when things are scarce and when non-payers can be excluded, not when things are plentiful or where non-payers cannot be kept out.

People are beginning to see, however, that there can be markets in environmental goods too. Rather than allow sea fish stocks to be harvested to destruction, for example, a number of countries now set a sustainable limit and issue permits to harvest part of that total. The permits are tradable, and a market quickly emerges, promoting efficiency while keeping stocks high.

And as people grow richer, thanks to the free-market economy, they can afford to take more care with their environment. China suffers severe pollution from its industries, but people there value basic economic growth more than the luxury of clean air. As they grow richer, like every rich country before them, standards will change and they will be able to afford cleaner industrial processes that pollute much less.

goes on in a free economy than in a centrally controlled one – it just happens to be done at the level of individuals rather than at the level of the state.

State-sponsored enterprises

Few states today believe that they can effectively own and manage the entire productive activity of their nation. Most of the world's economies are 'mixed' economies in which governments own only some industries and attempt to direct and manage the output of others through planning, regulations, subsidies, taxes and state shareholdings.

The twentieth century saw many countries nationalising industrial sectors that were said to be of particular strategic importance, and many countries continue to own and control these industries – which can include telecommunications, transport, banking, utilities, mining and much else.

Unfortunately, state ownership of such industries almost always creates a government monopoly. Such monopolies are often far too big for anyone to manage effectively. But it does not matter whether a monopoly is public or private; it will invariably become bloated and lazy and provide a poor service at a high cost.

The strategic importance of these industries is still no reason why the state has to own them. The banks of most of the richest countries are private: indeed, turning them into a state monopoly would soon ruin the banks and the businesses and families that rely on them. Commercial companies, operating as suppliers to the government or dealing directly with consumers, now provide much of the world's telecommunications, transport and utilities. Many countries have privatised their state-owned companies, recognising that these important services can be delivered better by competitive firms that can bring in private management expertise and private capital.

Governments have learned, however, that they can control industries without owning them. They might simply buy a stake in an important (and nominally privately owned) company, and use their rights as shareholders to control what the company does and who gets appointed to the board. Sometimes they give themselves 'golden shares' that give them the final say on key issues.

Such creeping interference would be rejected in a free society. It amounts to state ownership and expropriation, allowing governments to make decisions for the industry without having to purchase it. The owners – including ordinary people who may invest their savings and pensions in blue-chip companies – are effectively robbed of their property. And the opportunities for corruption are rife – cronies can be rewarded with lucrative board positions, factories can be located in favoured areas, and output can be used to benefit supporters.

Governments can also take effective control of private companies through regulation. Regulations can limit or dictate how companies operate, what they produce, how much they can charge, where they can invest and create jobs, how much they have to pay their workers – and much else. This sort of state control of private resources is very common, even in countries that call themselves free – but it is completely contrary to the principle of private property that is an essential foundation of a genuinely free society.

International trade
Trade versus protectionism

The benefits that arise from free commerce between individuals in the same country are also generated when people trade across international borders. Trade allows nations to specialise in what they do best, and send their surpluses to countries that are better placed to do other things. A large proportion of the world's cut flowers, for example, originate in Kenya, where the soil and climate are good for growing them; while Chile, Australia and France are known as leading wine producers because of their land and climate conditions and the expertise they have built up. India, with its relatively cheap but well-educated workforce, has become an important country for IT services and production. International trade allows people to specialise and build up capital such as tools and equipment to make their production more cost-effective.

And because the values of people in different countries probably differ more profoundly than the values of people in the same country, the potential opportunities for mutual gain through trade are that much greater. In medieval times, for example, European travellers would pay huge prices for products such as tea that grew easily and plentifully in India and China, or for spices that were cheap and commonplace in the Middle East. Today, people fly halfway round the world to visit the architecture of Venice or the culture of Thailand, marvelling at how different they are from their home countries.

A free society is open to products from all countries. It recognises the dynamic benefits from trade, and how trade helps spread prosperity. The alternative is protectionism, whereby countries attempt to protect their own suppliers by keeping out imports from other countries. This gives the domestic suppliers an easy time. But it means domestic consumers are denied better or cheaper goods and services that come from abroad. They pay higher prices to the protected domestic producers, have less choice and have to put up with poorer products.

Protectionism is waste

When a country produces something at home that could be produced better or cheaper abroad, it wastes resources (including environmental resources). Adam Smith pointed out that by means of greenhouses, grapes could be cultivated in cold, rainy Scotland – but at about thirty times the expense of growing them in the natural sunshine of France. Why waste resources – your time, money and effort – on trying to do something yourself when someone else does it better or more cheaply?[4]

Not surprisingly, efficient producers resent other countries trying to keep out their products through prohibitions, quotas and tariffs. They may well retaliate by raising barriers of their own. Such trade wars benefit nobody. It is much better – particularly for the poorest residents of both countries, who have most to gain from cheaper imports – if all barriers are removed and people are allowed to trade as they choose.

The same goes for immigration. In a free society the government would not place barriers on people moving between countries. Immigrants bring energy and new ideas that benefit the country they move to. Waves of immigration in Europe and to North America, for example, created enormous prosperity. Abandoning controls that have been in place for decades may not be easy, and may cause huge temporary problems: but it should remain an ultimate objective for believers in a free society.

Free trade in practice

Countries with open trading regimes grow faster and become

---

4   Adam Smith, *The Wealth of Nations*, 1776, Book IV, ch. II.

more prosperous than those without. Consider small trading cities such as Hong Kong and Singapore – neither of which has many natural resources to help them. In the 1960s, they were as poor as many African and Caribbean countries that had enormous resources. Today, thanks to trade and economic freedom, they are many times richer.

The spread of trade has reduced world poverty on a huge scale. Some people fear that allowing in imports, and foreign investment in particular, will lead to the exploitation of local populations – such as 'sweatshops' producing shoes or clothing. The truth is that nobody forces anyone to work in factories; but most people much prefer work in factories for a regular wage to backbreaking labour in the fields under a hot sun for an uncertain and lower reward. In countries such as Vietnam, where foreign investment has come in, those factory workers can now aspire to owning motor scooters, televisions and other luxuries that they had not dreamed of before.

Almost any sophisticated product today – such as a mobile phone or handheld computer – involves resources, skills and expertise gathered from all over the world. The designers might live in California, but the manufacture may well be managed by people in Hong Kong and done by others in China. Metals and other materials used in the product may be mined from Asia, Australia or South America. The products may be transported by shipping lines based in Greece or airlines based in the Netherlands. And the users, of course, are all over the world.

As people trade with those in other countries, they come to understand them better, or at least to respect them. Traders cannot afford to imagine themselves superior to those of other nations or races. To benefit themselves, they have to trade peacefully with others as suppliers or collaborators or customers. International trade generates understanding and peace, which has its own, wider, benefits. It is no surprise that the most free and open societies are those that have the most free and open trade.

6 PROPERTY AND JUSTICE

In Chapter 4 we saw that 'justice' has a very specific meaning – how people should behave with respect to each other, rather than how the rewards of their actions should be distributed between them. But the rules that govern the way that individuals behave towards each other are complex. Preserving and enforcing these rules of conduct requires certain values and social institutions – things such as property, the rule of law and respect for other people's rights.

Private property
The meaning of property

People's ability to own property is fundamental to the operation of a free society. Property ownership means that you are able to hold and control something, and – crucially – that you are entitled to exclude others from it. You can enjoy it, rent it out, sell it, give it away or even destroy it, but other people cannot use it or take it from you without your permission. Your property cannot legitimately be removed from you.

Individuals can own property, but so can groups, such as married couples, business partnerships and corporations, and governments and public bodies.

Property is not always something physical and immovable such as a piece of land or a building. It can be something movable, such as a farm animal, a truck or an item of clothing. It can be something non-physical too. It may be *intellectual property* such as a trademark or the copyright on something you have written or recorded, or patents on something you have designed. It can include shares in a company, a debt that somebody owes you, or your savings. It may be a lease to occupy someone else's land for a specified time or the right of a radio station to use a certain frequency. Property, then, is not necessarily something fixed and physical.

Property can be *created* too. A truck or an item of clothing is assembled out of component parts to make a new item of property. A farm animal is bred and nurtured to maturity. People write new books, or develop new savings packages. Digital technology has allowed the creation of huge numbers of mobile phone channels – a completely new form of property.

Importantly, your property also includes your rights over your own body and your right to enjoy the fruits of your own labour. In a free society, you cannot be arrested and imprisoned without good reason. You cannot legitimately be forced to work for someone else. Nor are others allowed to steal what you have created through your own skill, talent, knowledge or effort.

Property and progress

The institution of private property is as old as humanity, though it has not always been respected. In ancient Sparta, the idea of personal property was scorned. More recently, countries such as Russia and China experimented with collective ownership of farms and factories. But it was only with the gradual acceptance of private property, and its protection, that modern trade emerged

– bringing an enormous increase in wealth among the trading nations.

It is easy to see why. The ecologist Garrett Hardin wrote of 'the tragedy of the commons'.[1] When people own a resource, they are far more interested in preserving and nurturing it than if they do not. Land owned privately is better cultivated than that farmed collectively. The common stairwells and landings of apartment blocks are often dirty and dilapidated, though the individual apartments may be beautifully kept. People do not see why they should spend time and effort on something that does not belong to them, since other people would reap the benefits even if they did not do any of the work.

The protection of property and the respect for property ownership allow people to build up productive capital. Farmers are more likely to plant seed, cultivate crops and purchase tractors if they own the harvest that results. Entrepreneurs are more likely to take the risk of investing in factories, equipment and production networks if they can decide for themselves how that property is used and know that others have no right to take it. If property rights are protected and respected, people build up productive capital and productivity then grows, which helps the whole society. But if property can be stolen or destroyed by others, or someone else can take the things it produces, there is no incentive for people to invest their skill, time, money, effort and expertise in production – and the whole society suffers.

---

1   Garrett Hardin, 'The tragedy of the commons', *Science*, 162(3859), 1968, pp. 1243–8.

Property and other rights

The rights and freedoms that people enjoy in a free society are anchored in the institution of property. Without private property there can be no rights and no freedom.

Take, for example, the right of people to speak freely, to associate with others, and to take part in the political process. If there were no private property – say, if some government controlled all resources – how could candidates mount an election campaign? To communicate their message, they would need to hire meeting halls, print leaflets and broadcast their views. But if the government owned all the meeting places, controlled the supply of print and paper, and ran the broadcast media, it could effectively stop anyone's campaign.[2] (Indeed, if the candidate was critical of the government or its policies, the chance of that happening seems very high.) Worse still, if people had no property in their own person, there would be nothing to stop the government from silencing its critics by arresting or even murdering them. (It is shocking, but examples of this are all too common.)

Without property, there is no justice. Unless you have rights over your own body, your labour and your possessions, they can be taken from you without redress. If you have no right to your body, you can be arbitrarily arrested, imprisoned and murdered; if you have no right to your labour, you can be enslaved; if you have no right to your possessions, you can be robbed. There would be no protection from injustice.

---

2   A point made well in F. A. Hayek, *The Road to Serfdom*, Routledge, London, 1944.

Moral benefits of property

Property, and the protection of property rights, gives individuals a crucial buffer against the power of government and the coercion of others. Owning property gives individuals the ability to protect themselves, and to make their own choices, fashion their own plans, pursue their own ambitions or express their own views, without being subjected to the arbitrary will of others, either governments or individuals.

Property, and the rules of trade and exchange that grow from it, also allows individuals to cooperate peacefully to their mutual advantage. It enables them to live alongside each other and share both natural resources and the fruits of their labour according to agreed rules, without disputes, violence and coercion.

Not only does property promote peaceful cooperation; it makes cooperation a *necessity* for anyone who wants to better their own condition. People cannot simply take what they want by force. Property can be transferred – sold, rented, shared, leased out, or given away – only with the consent of the owner. The more-free societies have strong mechanisms to protect this important right, such as the rules on paying debts and honouring contracts. Free people regard this as a more moral way of transferring resources than their being taken by force or stolen through fraud.

A stake in society

It is not only those who own property who benefit from all this. By promoting investment, capital creation and trade, the whole society benefits. For example, city dwellers with no land of their own are fed thanks to farmers' incentive to nurture their crops and trade them voluntarily with customers. That is thanks to farmers' rights of ownership in their land and their crops. And the outcome is in striking contrast to countries in which property rights have not been protected – for example, in Robert Mugabe's Zimbabwe, where people were encouraged to occupy the land of the established farmers as their own. As the (mostly white) farmers fled, the result was not greater prosperity, but less: without clear landownership rules, production plummeted and city dwellers found themselves desperately short of food.

In a free society, the protection of people's property rights is therefore an important duty of government. It helps individuals protect themselves from coercion by criminals and by powerful or wealthy elites. The institution of private property gives everyone a stake in society and an interest in peaceful cooperation. Everyone gains from property rights that encourage owned resources to be well managed and efficiently used, allowing productive capital to be built up and maintained. Property ownership in a free society is not a special privilege of the few. It is open to everyone and it benefits everyone.

The rules of justice
Finding justice

Justice refers to the rules by which rewards and punishments are given out. It is based on our common human feelings of what people deserve as a result of their actions. If an individual deliberately harms others, for example, most human beings agree that they should compensate the victim and face punishment for their crime.

The rules of justice are not something that we can make up for ourselves. They are part of our very nature. Some people believe that this 'natural law' is given to us by our Creator and is revealed to us through our religion. Others, such as the Nobel economist and philosopher F. A. Hayek, take an evolutionary view, arguing that the rules of justice have grown up with us because they help us to live together peacefully as social creatures. Either way, it seems that we have natural feelings of justice that help promote cooperation and a well-functioning human society. If we had no such feelings and felt no injustice – if we took no action when people were robbed or murdered, say – we would not survive long.

The legislature and judiciary of a free society therefore cannot dictate what justice should be. Any rules they could dream up are unlikely to work better than those that are part of our nature. All they can hope to do is to *discover* what the rules of justice are.[3]

One can see this in the operation of common law or local legal systems. Disputes between individuals – boundary disputes between neighbours, for example – are brought to court. The court has to decide what outcome would be just, given the particular circumstances of the case. A second boundary dispute may be similar in some ways but not in others, and the court has to make another attempt to find the just outcome. The judges do not arbitrarily come to a decision. They apply long-accepted principles to new situations. And through a long process of testing like this, there gradually emerges a common understanding of what behaviour between neighbours is considered just and what is considered unjust.

---

3   This point is made in F. A. Hayek, *The Mirage of Social Justice*, University of Chicago Press, Chicago, IL, 1978.

Justice is not law, morality or equality

A fundamental feature of the rules of justice in a free society is that they should apply equally to everyone. Different people in the same circumstances should be treated the same way.

Laws and justice are not always the same thing. For example, laws may not always treat people equally. They may be created by elites precisely in order to help friends and harm enemies. These are *unjust* laws.

Nor are justice and morality the same thing. Many people might regard premarital sex as highly immoral. But that does not make it unjust. Nobody else is harmed by consensual actions like these; so under the no-harm rule, it is not just to inflict punishment on those who undertake them. Again, laws that do so are unjust laws. If the law can punish people merely because others find their behaviour offensive, there would be no freedom left for any of us.

Equality, likewise, is not the same as justice. The fact that some people are rich and others poor does not make a society unjust. An unequal society can be every bit as just as an equal one. Provided that people gain their property legitimately and without coercion, they act entirely justly.

Some critics of private property say that property can have originated only in theft. This is not true. The first people who might have staked a claim to a tract of unused and unwanted wilderness did no harm to anyone else. If they then benefited by farming it or discovering precious minerals under it, that was their good fortune: nobody else was left worse off, so no injustice was done. Similarly, if an entrepreneur invents a new product or process, and becomes wealthy from selling it to willing buyers, nobody has been harmed: on the contrary, the whole world benefits from the innovation.

The enforcement of justice

A key aim of a free society is to minimise the use of force. But justice has to be enforced somehow. If people harm others, we expect them to be punished, say with a fine or imprisonment. That means using force against the criminal. If justice is to prevail, some coercion is inevitable.

A free society resolves this dilemma by giving the monopoly on coercion to the civil authorities. Only they can use force, and even then only for the enforcement of justice and the protection of citizens from internal and external enemies. The use of force by other individuals is forbidden.

If the government is to have a monopoly on force, it must be strictly limited. Governments are made up of human beings, and no human being can be trusted to wield coercive power dispassionately. The temptation to use it for self-interest is too great.

Accordingly, the justice system of a free society incorporates strict rules that limit the coercive power of the authorities. For example, there must be strong rules on the authorities' powers of investigation and arrest, on how cases are tried, and on how punishments are meted out. These *procedural* rules are about *how* decisions are made, not about *what* is decided. These rules must be followed in order for the judicial process to be considered fair and just.

Threats to justice

This framework needs to be robust if individuals are not to be persecuted unjustly by the coercive power of the authorities. It is easily undone, even by people who think they are acting in the interests of justice. Judges, for example, sometimes think that their job is to create a fair outcome rather than to follow the procedural rules. But such *judicial activism* places judges' personal opinions above justice. It also makes the outcome of judicial proceedings unpredictable: the same offence could be given different punishments, depending on the particular judge. And it gives those in power greater influence over judicial outcomes: if they can bribe or intimidate the judges, they can change people's punishments. But if there are firm procedural rules that must be followed in every case, such influence is curbed. This is a crucial protection for those who come before the courts.

Another approach that undermines the administration of justice is the idea of 'social justice'. The deliberate creation of a more equal distribution of wealth and income is at odds with the principles of property and justice. To create the equal distribution, property has to be taken from some people and given to others. The rules of ownership, which give people the right to hold property and dispose of it as they choose, have to be torn up. Again, once we give authorities such sweeping power, nobody is safe. Enterprise will be thwarted, too: why should anyone take risks or expend effort to acquire property, if the authorities can confiscate it?

The precise rules that should apply to property ownership are not always obvious, however. Does my ownership of a piece of land give me the right to exploit the minerals underneath it? Does it allow me to forbid people flying over it in an aircraft? Can I prevent a nearby factory polluting my air with a smoky chimney? These details have to be determined.[4] And in a free society they are, by being continually tested and refined in the courts, by

---

4   This point is raised by Milton Friedman and Rose Friedman, *Capitalism and Freedom*, University of Chicago Press, Chicago, IL, 1962.

dispassionate judges who attempt only to pinpoint what the rules of justice actually are.

Natural justice

In a free society, all law-making and law enforcement must follow principles of justice – principles so deeply rooted in our humanity that they are called *natural justice*.

Firstly, the law must be *known, clear and certain*. If a law is secret or keeps changing, individuals cannot know if they are breaking it, and so cannot protect themselves against prosecution.

Laws must also be *predictable*. Individuals should be able to work out where laws do and do not apply, and what the consequences of breaking them will be. Even in supposedly free societies, laws are often introduced for one purpose – such as to counteract terrorism or organised crime – and then are used for a completely different one. Citizens may find themselves facing severe penalties for what are in fact minor offences.

Secondly, laws cannot be *retrospective*. They can apply only to future actions. Otherwise, people can find themselves prosecuted for actions that were perfectly legal when they performed them. Again, supposedly free societies fail at this. For example, a 2008 United Kingdom law outlawing certain tax-avoidance schemes amended earlier legislation in ways that imposed a tax liability on 3,000 people who were not acting illegally at the time.

A third rule of justice is that the law cannot require individuals to do something *infeasible*, since that too would make it impossible for people to avoid breaking the law. Even supposedly free countries also fail this test, particularly where laws conflict: thus fire regulations may require an owner to install a fire escape on a building that planning laws forbid from being altered – so either way, the owner is breaking the law. More disturbing still, unjust governments may use deliberately infeasible laws to persecute their opponents.

Another key rule of natural justice is the *presumption of innocence*. Nobody can be treated like a guilty person until proved so, even if the case against them seems watertight. Crucially, that means it is up to the authorities to *prove their guilt*, not for them to prove their innocence. This makes it harder for governments to harass their enemies with trumped-up charges: all charges have to be proved in court before people can be punished.

A last key principle is that judges and courts should be *independent* of the political authorities. There needs to be a *separation of powers* between those who make the law and those who adjudicate on it. The judges must not be mere agents of the politicians: their political views should be irrelevant to how they handle cases. If judges are so close to politicians that they are easily influenced or intimidated by them, then the court system comes to serve political interests rather than genuine justice. The more-free societies often have independent panels to appoint judges, or appoint them for life, which reduces the leverage that politicians can exert over them.

The rule of law
Meaning of the rule of law

Nothing distinguishes a free from a non-free society more clearly than the rule of law. This is the idea that citizens should be governed by clear and general principles of law, rather than by the arbitrary whim of monarchs and politicians. Legislators cannot just do as they please. Their laws must apply equally to everyone, including themselves.

The purpose of the rule of law is to protect individuals against the exercise of arbitrary power. If we give governments the monopoly on force, we must ensure that it is used only for the purposes intended, predictably, with due accountability, and for the general benefit of the whole society, not some elite.

The rule of law also ensures that those in authority face the same criminal penalties for wrongdoing as everyone else. A disturbing number of countries grant their current and former government leaders immunity from prosecution – and a disturbing number of those leaders have escaped justice as a result. While there is a case for protecting public figures – and anyone else – from unfounded (or politically motivated) and vexatious prosecutions, there is no case for granting anyone immunity from genuine justice.

The rule of law, then, rests on general and enduring principles, rather than the changing and arbitrary decisions of rulers. It guarantees us natural justice through rules such as equality before the law, the due process of law, an independent judiciary, blind justice, habeas corpus (not being held for long periods without trial), not being harassed by the authorities (say, by being tried over and over again for the same offence – so-called *double jeopardy*), the presumption of innocence (such that you are not treated as guilty until actually convicted) and the certainty, stability and feasibility of laws. And crucially, those who make laws are bound by them along with everyone else. A society cannot be free if some people, however elevated, are not accountable for their actions.

Protecting the rule of law

Countries have different ways to prevent the rule of law being eroded by those in authority. These include written constitutions, a judicial process built on common law and precedent, and a basic commitment to natural justice.

Written constitutions can give strength to the rule of law. But it is much easier to create such a constitution at the birth of a new country, when citizens are coming together for the first time, rather than in a mature country, where elites and vested interests already have a grip on power and are likely to twist any new constitution to benefit themselves.

The rule of law can also be supported by years of precedent as different cases are taken to court. Individuals can object to the rulings of legislators and officials, and test their justice and legality in court. Gradually, a body of precedent marks out the limits of official power.

A third way of bolstering the rule of law is by promoting discussion on the rules of justice and the principles underpinning social harmony. If free speech prevails and anyone is free to discuss these ideas, it becomes much harder for the authorities to twist the understanding of them for their own advantage.

One key idea that comes out of discussions of the rule of law is that, if people were coming together for the first time to decide the principles by which they were to be governed, nobody would agree to be coerced by others, except in ways – such as punishments for theft or violence – that they would all see as being in their own long-term interests. So we might reasonably infer that all free societies *should* be based on general rules that limit coercion and prevent particular groups being able to exploit others.

Administration of justice

Whatever general routes are chosen to safeguard the rule of law, there are some specific measures that certainly help.

Judges must be personally, as well as politically, independent. Otherwise, the judicial system will not be respected, and huge injustices will be done in the name of justice. In many countries, judges are underpaid, unaccountable and poorly monitored: so they decide cases on the basis of bribes rather than the law. Instead, judges must be properly paid and regularly scrutinised so that such corruption is neither necessary nor tolerated.

The justice system also needs to be supported by a good court administration. In many countries it can take months or even years for even a small dispute to reach the courts because of the enormous bureaucracy involved and officials' lack of incentives to manage cases. A legal system based on precedent needs rapid access to past cases and judgements, so cases are not brought wastefully to court simply because there are no records of past precedents.

In many countries, the police are also part of the problem rather than the solution. Because of their power of arrest and detention, they can inflict great injustices on people and benefit themselves through corruption. Officers imposing small 'fines' for real or imagined minor traffic offences is symptomatic of this. It becomes part of the prevailing culture – but once the principle of bribery is accepted, there is no rule to prevent much worse things. Police need to be properly trained and monitored, ideally with an independent agency empowered to investigate and act on complaints against them.

Likewise the bureaucracy must be appointed on merit, rather than through political favours. They must be properly accountable. Taking decisions for political or personal gain should be punished.

Elections must be fairly run if justice and the rule of law are to prevail. There must be free speech so that candidates who are critical of the authorities can stand and put across their point of view. There must also be secret ballots and a genuinely independent election commission to ensure that electoral boundaries are drawn fairly and elections are conducted honestly.

Justice and economic progress

The rule of law is economically as well as socially important. Each year, the World Bank ranks countries in terms of the ease of doing business in them. Attracting business and investment from abroad, and making it easier for people to trade at home, is of course an important factor in the economic development and prosperity of the population. The index looks at the transparency of taxes and regulations, levels of corruption among officials, and how easily people can start a business, register property, trade across borders, deal with insolvencies, and so on.

Singapore, which is very free in economic terms (though much less free socially), has topped the global rankings for seven years, followed by other relatively free countries such as Hong Kong, New Zealand, Denmark, the United Kingdom and the United States. Next comes the Republic of Korea, another economically free but socially rather restricted country. At the bottom of the rankings come countries where justice and the rule of law are notoriously weak – such as Congo, Venezuela, Zimbabwe, Iraq, Cameroon, Bolivia and Uzbekistan.

Threats to the rule of law

In many countries, particularly developing countries, various systems of justice prevail. In addition to state-level laws and justice systems, there are often local, tribal or religious legal systems, as well as private or contract law between individuals.

Corruption is more likely in the state systems. The local, religious and private legal systems usually have much deeper roots in natural justice, and therefore more widespread acceptance. State systems, by contrast, were often imposed by colonial or occupying powers. They may never have had much acceptance, but their power and patronage remain for any corrupt person to exploit.

People in government and state judiciaries often see nothing wrong in exploiting state power. The military, police and officials take bribes. Politicians are almost expected to rob the state to benefit their local community, or even themselves. But what is regarded as wrong in personal life should be seen as wrong in the public sphere too.

In places where travel and communications are difficult and local issues are the most urgent and crucial ones, a mixture of systems may make sense. But the aim must be for all systems of justice to have the authority and consent of local laws, the clarity and principle of state laws, and the objectivity of the rule of law.

Human rights
Defining human rights

From such reflections on justice emerges the idea of *human rights*.[5] This is the idea that people are due basic freedoms by virtue of

---

5   For more on this, see Nigel Ashford, *Principles for a Free Society*, Jarl Hjalmarson Foundation, Stockholm, 2003.

their humanity – rights that, like natural law, promote the smooth working of society, but rights that are specifically acknowledged as *universal* (applying everywhere and to everyone) and *inalienable* (they cannot be given up, nor denied by others).

These human 'rights' might better be called human *freedoms*. They include such freedoms as owning property, self-determination and self-ownership of your own body and labour, freedom to move and locate where you choose, and freedom to practise your own religion. Their effect is to limit the state in how it can treat people.

Unfortunately, 'human rights' are often confused with legal rights that are delivered through the political structure, or with social and cultural norms. But laws giving workers paid holidays, for example, are not human rights because they are not *universal*. They apply only to workers and only in countries where such luxuries are affordable. And they can be *alienated* – a worker can give up holiday entitlement in exchange for money, without losing any freedom. Likewise, laws on equal pay for men and women are not human rights because they are not a claim to human freedom but a coercive demand on employers.

Group rights are not human rights either. They do not apply universally. The special treatment given to, say, the native peoples of America are merely legal privileges: other people do not enjoy them. Something cannot be a 'human' right if it focuses not on people's humanity but on their membership of some special group.

Freedoms, rights and duties

It is important to be clear about such issues. Confusing human rights with social norms and legal privileges gives a false authority to the latter and undermines the whole idea of the former. While some things – equal pay, paid holidays or even special recognition of some disadvantaged group – may be desirable, the fact is that not everything that is desirable is a human right.

Human 'rights' guarantee our freedom – they do not put coercive demands on anyone else. Freedom of speech, for example, imposes no obligation or duty on anyone else, other than the obligation or duty to respect it. Nobody is required to provide you with a newspaper column or a radio show so that your views can be broadcast, nor to help make sure that you do actually speak freely, nor even to listen to what you might say.

By contrast, the United Nations Declaration of Human Rights lists the 'right' to free education. But free education is not a human right because this implies that other people are obliged to pay for it. The provision of education has a cost – time, effort, materials and money are all spent in providing it. In a truly free society, nobody can have a *right* to enjoy an education free of charge, because that would put an *obligation* on other people to provide those resources. (Of course, many people might be perfectly willing to share the cost: but a free society cannot *compel* them to.)

Too often, people talk about *rights* without mentioning, or even recognising, the implied obligations on others, the compulsion that is needed to enforce them, and the wider damage that this compulsion creates.

Once again, there is no *right* to welfare in free societies: that would imply that some people have an obligation to support others, when the only obligation is to do them no harm. But this does not mean that poor or disabled people fare any worse than in a welfare culture. The tax costs of welfare might discourage work and enterprise, making the whole society poorer, and welfare benefits may encourage dependency. And the philanthropic bodies in a rich, free society might well support those in need better than bureaucratic government agencies.

7 THE SPONTANEOUS SOCIETY

Order without commands

A free society can run itself without needing a large state. That may sound surprising, but human life abounds with examples. As the American economist Daniel B. Klein observes, you might think that a roller-skating rink – with perhaps a hundred or more people from toddlers to grandparents, with wheels strapped to their shoes but no helmets, knee pads or skating qualifications, all going round a hard floor at different speeds – would be a series of accidents waiting to happen. But, in fact, skaters manage to navigate their way round the rink, avoiding others, without any need for official speed limits, turn signals and stop lights.[1] It does not require some planner or policing agency to tell them where and how fast to skate. By each looking out for themselves, plus a little common courtesy to others, they achieve their mutual interests of having fun while avoiding collisions.

Even more impressively, human language is highly structured and hugely beneficial to us, though it has not been consciously designed by any authority. The rules of grammar that make language work have grown up quite naturally over the centuries, because they enable us to understand each other. We follow these

---

1   Daniel B. Klein, 'Rinkonomics: A window on spontaneous order', Online Library of Liberty (Articles), 2006.

rules even though they are subtle and complex and we would have difficulty writing them down. No government commission could ever create rules of such complexity, subtlety and effectiveness. They have simply evolved with us.

Many parts of human society work like this. Without having to be told how to behave by officials, we nevertheless act in orderly, regular, predictable ways, simply by following a few basic rules that we have grown up with as part of our nature. By following them, we create vast and hugely beneficial social orders. The simple rules that allow us to trade peacefully together, for example, have created the international market economy through which the whole world cooperates.

Rule-guided societies

The interpersonal rules of a free society give people much more latitude than they have in a government-controlled society. Free individuals can do any of the many things that are not specifically forbidden, rather than being limited to the few things that the authorities specifically permit. This means that free societies can be a lot more flexible and adaptive, responding easily to changing circumstances rather than having to wait for orders.

These rules – such as the rules of ownership and property in a market economy – embody a kind of wisdom, discovered over the years, about what works and what does not. They adapt and change as circumstances change, reflecting the lessons of trial and error over many years and millions of human interactions. They include behavioural norms about how to treat other people, legal norms that attempt to express the natural law in writing, and common law that is built up over a large number of test cases.

This rule-guided, spontaneous society is not only more creative and adaptive; it can be far more complex than one directed from the centre. Like language, it can be so complicated that none of us can even describe all its rules – and yet still work very well. A society based on the commands of some authority is inevitably limited, in both size and nature, to what those few in authority can get their minds round. But a society based on rules that have been built up as a result of millions of human interactions over thousands of years contains a much broader and deeper wisdom. The centrally directed society relies on the limited wisdom of a few; the rule-guided society encapsulates the wisdom of multitudes.

Hence the mistake often made by government authorities, that they could plan out a society or an economy better and more rationally than the everyday rules of social and economic interaction. By discarding and twisting the wisdom contained in this complex rule system, they invariably make things worse.

Dispersed knowledge and power

The inherent wisdom of the spontaneous, rule-guided society does not exist at some centre. It is held by millions of individuals as they go about their everyday lives. Since power is dispersed, those individuals can try their own, small-scale experiments in living. They can take risks and chances that threaten nobody but themselves. But if those risks pay off, they are available for everyone to adopt and benefit from. That promotes experimentation and adaptation to changing circumstances, giving the spontaneous society a greater chance of success in a world of change. Government authorities, by contrast, take decisions for everyone, and thereby risk everyone's lives and fortunes. So they have to act more conservatively than do free individuals – or risk making massive mistakes. And as a result, non-free societies adapt less quickly and successfully.

Of course, the spontaneous society and economy can never be perfect. They are the product of human action (though not human design) and human beings are never perfect. We cannot predict the future, for example, so we make errors in our attempts to adapt to it. And the information that each of us has is inevitably partial and local. But in a world of free human interaction, this partial and local information drives a remarkably intelligent and adaptive society and economy.

In a free society, people have to find out for themselves how best to adapt to other people – who are in turn trying to adapt to the actions of everyone else. It is rather like a busy railway station at rush hour when everyone is trying to make their way to one of many exits, or coming in at one of a number of entrances and trying to get to their particular train. They each have an eye to where they are going, though their route there will probably not be at all direct. They will have to weave around other people, all of whom are trying to do the same, changing direction as others step into their path. It might look like chaos, but in fact everybody gets to their destination without conflict. If some authority had to tell each of the hundreds or thousands of people in the station exactly where and when to move, it would be hours or days before any of them got anywhere. The problem is far too complicated to be solved centrally. But the spontaneous society solves it easily and in real time.

Toleration

The meaning of toleration

In this way, people in a free society each have to adapt to the actions of others. So it is important that people show toleration towards others – including those whose actions and lifestyles they disagree with or even find shocking.

In a free society we cannot prevent someone from doing something just because we dislike it. We could intervene only if their actions were causing or were likely to cause harm to others. John Stuart Mill was clear that this meant *physical* harm. If 'harm' included things such as shock, moral indignation or embarrassment, then almost every action could be forbidden and there would be no freedom at all. In any case, the moral outrage of those who wanted to forbid the behaviour would be matched by the moral outrage of those who resented their freedom to practise it being curbed. No matter how numerous or emotional each side might be, there is still no objective way to decide between them. And since a free society does not allow disputes to be settled by force, each side simply has to tolerate the opinions, behaviour and lifestyles of the other.

That is not the same as moral indifference. A parent who did not discourage the bad behaviour of a child would not be acting with toleration, but would be neglecting the child's moral education. If adults behave in ways that we regard as shocking, we have a perfect right to say so and to try to persuade them to act differently – though not to force them.

Nor is toleration the same as moral relativism – the idea that all morality is equally valid because people disagree about morality and there is no objective way to choose between them. We are perfectly entitled to believe that our own moral or religious codes are better than other people's – but not to force our ideas on anyone else.

Toleration, heterogeneity and choice

Tolerating others may be difficult when populations are becoming increasingly heterogeneous. Easier international travel, falling immigration barriers and our more globalised economy are only some of the reasons why the populations of many countries are far more diverse than they were a few decades ago.

Some people argue that greater choice will lead to the different racial, cultural, national, linguistic or religious groups becoming even more separate, stoking up tensions that would undermine toleration. For example, parents may want their children to grow up with others of the same race, and if they can choose their own schools there may be more chance of segregation than if children simply have to attend the school specified by the government authorities.

In reality, schools are likely to be *less* integrated when the government assigns school places, since children will usually be sent to the nearest school. And since people of the same ethnic group tend to live alongside each other, the school population will reflect this lack of mix. But if parents can choose schools, they may well choose schools in other neighbourhoods, or ones that select for some other characteristic that they value more highly than ethnicity, such as academic, musical or linguistic abilities.

Ethnic segregation is quite natural, and people tend to pick their friends and work colleagues from the same group. But there is every difference between that and being intolerant of other communities. The worst ethnic tensions are in places where some groups are denied the rights and advantages of others – in other words, when the basic principles of a free society are breached.

The fundamentalist threat to toleration

The biggest threat to toleration of others is moral, ideological or religious fundamentalism. Many people with strong religious views, say, might consider homosexuality or premarital sexual relations as disgusting, shameful, shocking or immoral. They might well consider things like sacrilege, making images of the deity, denying the religious texts, rejecting the moral code of the religion or adhering to some other religion as pure evil. This they would see as reason enough for such behaviours to be outlawed and punished.

But however much disgust or shock a person's actions create in others, and however evil they might be judged on religious grounds, no one has the power to prohibit them in a free society unless they physically harm others, or threaten to do so. Again, this does not stop members of the religion from criticising these actions and arguing against them, or excluding their practitioners from the religious community – provided that none of this turns into intimidation or actual harm. But nor does it allow anyone, including governments, to restrain, censor, arrest, imprison, torture, maim, exile or execute any person or group for these views and actions.

The founding texts of many of the world's religions embrace toleration of others, though in some cases the authorities have interpreted them differently for their own ends. Foreign powers that have occupied a territory have often occupied its religion too, diverting its moral and judicial codes into justifying and serving their own administration. Some totalitarian governments even attempted to suppress religion entirely, seeing it as a rival to their own ideology and power. But it does not matter in a free society whether the fundamentalism in question is religious or ideological. It still provides no authority to coerce others whose actions, morality, religion or ideology are different.

Political correctness

There is a more subtle threat to toleration: political correctness. This is where social and political pressure is put on individuals to accept the attitudes and opinions of some prevailing elite. Commonly, those who do not agree with the prevailing opinion are caricatured as deranged or wicked, the aim being to taint their opinions as deranged or wicked too. This allows those opinions to be conveniently dismissed rather than debated. It also suggests that the elite's views are more solid than they really are.

This process relies on a subtle form of coercion, in which those with different opinions are tainted so that they find it difficult to make their way through society. For example, academics who question the evidence for man-made climate change might be denied jobs or promotion in the universities. In a free society, employers are not bound to hire people they disagree with, of course; nor are the media obliged to report controversial theories. But where educational institutions or the media are government-run monopolies or near-monopolies, this exclusion of people with minority views amounts to real coercion.

Toleration and the quest for truth

Toleration in a free society goes well beyond the toleration of religious or ideological differences. For example, it includes freedom of expression – in speech, writing, broadcast or any other medium – which in turn implies the absence of censorship.

Some people may regard a world without censorship as deeply worrying. Many might be deeply shocked by the words, images, arguments and ideas that could be put forward in so free a world. But in a free society we have no right to prevent free speech and block people's opinions, even if nearly all of us disagree with what is said, find it offensive or believe it immoral.

There is, of course, a case for some curbs on free speech if what is said causes danger to others – such as shouting 'Fire!' in a theatre. We would legitimately punish someone who recklessly risked injury to others like this. Similarly, we protect children against words or images that we believe might corrupt them. We might not allow explicit advertisements for drugs, say, to appear on billboards near schools. And there is a strong case for giving people information – such as movie classifications – so that they do not stumble unwittingly across things that would distress them.

That is very different to outright censorship – preventing particular words, images, arguments and ideas from being aired at all. There can be no such censorship in a genuinely free society because a free society is based on openness and choice. People must know the options available to them if they are to choose rationally and try new ideas that might improve everyone's future. Censorship closes off those options and choices and thereby denies us progress.

Nor can we trust the censors. Truth and authority are two

different things. Those in power may have their own reasons – such as self-preservation – for forbidding certain ideas being broadcast. But even if the censors have the public's best interests at heart, they are not infallible. They have no monopoly of wisdom, no special knowledge of what is true and what is not. Only debate, argument and experience will determine that. The censors may suppress the truth simply by mistake. They can never be sure if they are stifling ideas that will eventually prove to be correct. Some ideas may be mostly wrong, and yet contain a measure of truth, which argument can eke out. The truth of other ideas may become obvious only over time.

The way to ensure that we do not stifle true and useful ideas is to allow all ideas to be aired, confident that their merits or shortcomings will be revealed through debate. That means allowing people to argue their case, even on matters that the majority regard as certainties. Truth can only be strengthened by such a contest. It was for this reason that, from 1587 until 1983, the Roman Catholic Church appointed a 'devil's advocate' to put the case against a person being nominated for sainthood. It is useful to expose our convictions to questioning. If we believe others are mistaken in their views, those views should be taken on and refuted, not silenced.

From Socrates onward, history is littered with examples of people who have been persecuted for their views. Such persecution often cows people into staying silent, even though their ideas are subsequently vindicated. Fearing the wrath of the Roman Catholic Church, Nicolaus Copernicus did not publish his revolutionary theory that the planets rotated about the sun until just before his death in 1543. His follower Galileo Galilei was tried by the Inquisition and spent his remaining days under house arrest.

Such intimidation suppresses truth, debate and progress. It harms society as well as the heretics who are persecuted.

If we simply accept prevailing ideas without allowing any argument, those ideas rest on a very insecure foundation. Their acceptance is uncritical. They become platitudes rather than meaningful truths. And when new ideas eventually do break through, it is likely to be violently and disruptively.

It can be unsettling when people say things with which we fundamentally disagree, express ideas we believe are profoundly wrong, do things we regard as deeply shocking, or even scorn our moral and religious beliefs. But our toleration of these things shows our commitment to freedom, and our belief that we make more progress, and discover new truths faster, by allowing different ideas to be debated rather than suppressed.

Prohibitions

We would be furious if many of the things that we enjoyed in our everyday existence were banned. Unfortunately, many of them already are.[2]

The no-harm rule says that we have no right to prevent actions unless they harm or risk harm to others. But many activities are banned on the grounds that they harm those who do them. This is the reasoning behind bans on drug-taking, smoking, alcohol and much more. The trouble is that the justification of saving people from harming themselves would allow just about any activity to be banned. It is too easy to argue that people are harmed or put at risk by drinking sugary drinks, eating fatty foods, taking part

---

2   For an excellent discussion of prohibitions, see John Meadowcroft (ed.), *Prohibitions*, Institute of Economic Affairs, London, 2008.

in dangerous sports, engaging in prostitution or homosexuality, adopting a different religion or questioning authority. Given the number of people who argue exactly these things, once the principle is lost it cannot take long for freedom itself to be suppressed.

Prohibitions often have practically damaging results too. By driving the demand for certain things underground, they become more difficult to monitor and control, and criminals may move in to supply them. The United States, for example, still suffers from the presence of a criminal mafia whose power grew in the Prohibition years of a century ago, when supplying alcohol was a criminal offence. The continued illegality of gambling and prostitution in most parts of the USA has further promoted such criminal elements, who are happy to supply these services to meet the demand for them.

Prohibitions also make it more difficult for people to understand the effects of their behaviour. People still demand drugs, but if drugs are illegal it becomes harder to get good information about their dangers. It is also hard for users to check the quality of what they are buying. It becomes difficult for people who do become dependent on drugs to seek medical or social help, since to do so is to admit their own criminality. And people become exposed to other risks, such as the risk of AIDS contracted through unsterilised needles, because the illegality of drugs makes it impossible to take them in a safe environment. The result is that much if not most of the harm that drugs do is due to the fact that they are illegal.[3]

Prohibitions like these criminalise otherwise honest people who see no harm in taking recreational drugs, or gambling, or drinking alcohol at home with friends, none of which harms other

---

3   A point made strongly in Milton Friedman and Rose Friedman, *Capitalism and Freedom*, Chicago University Press, Chicago, IL, 1962.

Question: Don't we have to protect people from themselves?

No. Do you want to be 'protected' from yourself? Or do you think you should make your own decisions about how to live your life? Allowing governments to decide what is good and bad for us is inefficient: we are in a much better position than distant officials to judge the risks we take. And it is dangerous: governments may start by banning things that everyone agrees are harmful, but once the principle is conceded, they can ban everything.

Should we be prevented from snorting cocaine, smoking tobacco, drinking alcohol, eating fatty food or swigging sugary drinks? Should we be forced by law to take exercise, give up dangerous sports and attend church? Should we be barred from reading 'dangerous' books or from criticising our rulers? The answer in a free society is *no*. If people are offending our morals or doing something dangerous, we should tell them so. But as long as they are doing no harm to anyone else, we have no right to stop them.

people at all. And having flouted the law with trivial offences, they may go on to risk more serious and potentially harmful ones.

Prohibitions almost never work. Alcohol prohibition in the United States merely drove drinking underground to where it could not be controlled. Strict drug laws and large penalties for drug dealing around the world have not prevented a trade that is estimated to be worth many hundreds of *billions* of dollars.

Trying to eradicate commonplace behaviour is wasteful. And it is a threat to freedom because a massive monitoring and enforcement apparatus is needed if it is to make any impact at all. That simply diverts law enforcement resources from the investigation and prosecution of genuinely harmful offences. It also opens up opportunities for corruption among the police and the courts; even though little or no harm may be done to others by gambling or drug-taking, the penalties may be large, enabling officials to extract large bribes from those involved in them.

Public and private behaviour

The rules of a free society govern *public* behaviour – how individuals behave with respect to others. But *private* behaviour – affecting only the individual concerned – remains in the private sphere. It becomes a legal matter only if it causes harm to others.

Yet in a free society it is necessary to be very careful that the actual harm or risk of harm is genuine. Should people be permitted to sell poisons? Given that poisons have many uses that do not involve harm to humans, more harm might be done by banning their sale than permitting it. There may well be a case for logging the names of those who sell and buy poisons, so that poisoners know that they are likely to be detected; but no more than that.[4]

Should there be a rule against public drunkenness? Or against the operation of brothels or gambling houses? Yes, if they cause violence, which is why many countries choose to license them. But for the most part, these activities affect only the people concerned. Other people might be disgusted by the thought of them, but if we allow activities to be banned on the grounds of anything but

---

4   This and the following points are made well in John Stuart Mill, *On Liberty*, 1859, in John Stuart Mill, *On Liberty and other Essays*, Oxford University Press, Oxford, 2008.

objective harm caused to other people, no human activity is safe from the moralists.

Should people be permitted to trade on holy days? Or engage in polygamy? It is their own business, not ours; it does no harm to anyone else. The laws of a free society exist to preserve and expand the freedom of individuals, not to impose the morality of some people on others.

Nevertheless, in a free society people are allowed to set their own rules on their own property, provided that the no-harm rule is not broken. In many countries, some public spaces (such as shopping malls) are privately owned rather than controlled by the political authorities. Thus in 2005 the Bluewater shopping centre in south-east England banned swearing, smoking, leafleting and wearing clothes that obscure the face (such as hooded tops). In Bournville, central England – the factory town created by chocolate-maker George Cadbury and run by a private trust that remains true to his principles – the open sale of alcohol is not permitted. Since Bluewater and Bournville are private property, they are fully within their rights.

The problem of altruism

Many people are disturbed by the thought that free societies and free economies operate on the basis of the self-interest of those involved. They would prefer a world that was driven instead by altruism – a selfless concern for the interest and wellbeing of others. But this leads to even more problems than it solves.[5]

---

5   For a fuller explanation of this, see Mao Yushi, 'The paradox of morality', in Tom G. Palmer, *The Morality of Capitalism*, Students for Liberty and Atlas Foundation, Arlington, VA, 2011.

No guide for helping others

How, for a start, can we ever know what is in the interest of other people? We have no direct access to their minds and values. If we were trying to do what was in their interest, we would surely make major mistakes. Anyone who has ever received a completely inappropriate birthday present knows how even family and friends can be poor judges of a person's taste. The giving culture seems an inefficient basis on which to run a whole society.

It is also hard to be critical of the things that other people give us. We accept gifts with seeming gratitude, even if we hate them. This means that people in an altruistic society would never learn exactly what others really want. That is in stark contrast to an economy built on self-interest, where if customers do not get exactly what they want from a supplier, they say so, and threaten to take their business elsewhere. Self-interest focuses suppliers on giving people exactly the right products as cheaply as possible.

Altruism produces conflict

If deliberately trying to help others was what motivated business transactions, there would be just as much tension between buyers and sellers as there is in today's world of self-interest. Buyers would demand higher prices in order to benefit the sellers. Sellers would pitch prices low to maximise the benefit to the buyers. It is just the mirror image of what happens today.

In a market economy, self-interested people are in conflict with each other, but they can resolve their conflicts by bargaining. If the only motive were to benefit others, there would be no way to resolve conflicts. Each altruist would insist on making the other better off. Since neither wants to gain from the deal, the urgency of their own needs would not help them to agree.

Self-interest and cost–benefit

Self-interest focuses providers – and customers too – on making sure that the benefits of a transaction exceed its costs. An altruistic supplier who worked for no reward would send out a very misleading signal to everyone – the signal that their time and expertise had zero cost. Customers, taking this signal at face value, would soon overwhelm the suppliers with their demand. Suppliers would have no way to refuse to provide a service, even if its benefit was marginal or was dwarfed by the cost.

Leatherworkers, for example, would face endless lines of people with goods to repair. In the self-interested market economy, such traders would tell customers point-blank if their goods were not worth repairing; or else they would quote a price so high that the customer would decide not to bother. The market manages demand, and focuses effort on what is really worthwhile.

In an altruistic world, people would be rushing to help neighbours with all sorts of tasks – building a house, say. But in practical and cost-effectiveness terms, it might be better for the neighbour to go to the marketplace and hire a professional house builder, rather than rely on the unskilled labour of friends. The loss is compounded if those neighbours could use their talents more effectively in other kinds of work. The market encourages people to put their time and skills where they are most valued.

Question: Shouldn't we control prices so poor people can afford things?

No. Prices are signals of scarcity. They tell us where there are surpluses and shortages. They tell producers that more of a product is needed, and consumers that they should cut back or look for alternatives. Price controls suppress these signals and so demand outstrips supply and there are shortages. This commonly leads to rationing of the scarce products, which is even less efficient.

An example is rent controls, designed to make housing affordable. What they actually do is make housing worse or unavailable, as owners decide the rents they get are not worth their while, and take their property off the rental market. If some people cannot afford essentials, the best solution is not to interfere with the market mechanism, but to give them money – either through private charity or through a tax-funded minimum income scheme. Then they can buy these things in the same efficient and competitive market as everyone else.

The morality of the marketplace

The fact that a free-market economy is based on self-interest does not make it immoral. In markets, people can prosper only by cooperating with others by supplying the things that they want. Anti-social behaviour is punished: why should anyone trade with a rude misanthrope when there are plenty of more agreeable people out there, willing to do business?

There are also rules to make sure that markets work smoothly without coercion. But formal rules cannot deal with every specific case. Markets inevitably rely on trust, and they reward those who have a reputation for being trustworthy and reliable. Even though the driving force is self-interest, markets promote a mutually beneficial morality.

Corporate social responsibility

Many people want businesses to act more morally, and promote 'corporate social responsibility'. Many large international businesses now publish annual reports explaining what they are doing to be good citizens.

But only *individuals* can be responsible or irresponsible, moral or immoral. *Groups* have no separate morality of their own. A country, a town, a race, a tribe, a club or a company cannot be moral or immoral – only its individual members. Certainly, we would like business leaders to build a moral culture in their organisations. But morality and responsibility are reflected in actions – and actions are taken by individuals, not groups.

The corporate social responsibility movement is actually an attempt to pass the cost of civic and welfare programmes on to business. Businesses try to show how responsible they are by funding local schools, community groups and so on. It may make good business sense for them to do this: after all, they have to recruit from the local schools and a positive relationship with them could make recruitment easier. But this should be a business decision made willingly by executives and shareholders, not forced upon them in the name of ethics.

If business were properly competitive, there would in any case be no spare cash to support local projects that did not serve the commercial prospects of the business. If firms have money to spare on such projects, it is an indication that the market is not working (for example, government regulation is protecting the companies from competition). In a truly competitive market, those firms would lose out to others who scrapped the window-dressing local projects, and skimmed off the resultant profits.

Nor are business people particularly good at making sure the money they devote to community projects is in fact well spent. They would be better advised to concentrate on their core role of earning profits by providing the goods and services that people really want – which in turn would generate the general wealth that makes philanthropy affordable.

8 PRIVATISATION AND GLOBALISATION

Migration and technology
A world opening up

Once-remote corners of the planet are no longer remote. Television, radio, the internet and other communications bring other cultures, lifestyles, races, people, countries and systems of government closer to us. Air travel and faster land transport make it possible to visit more places first-hand.

This has made it harder for governments to conceal their faults. There is no longer any point in a government building a wall around its territory in the hope of keeping its citizens ignorant of its own shortcomings. Thanks to daily contact with the rest of the world through social media or foreign TV captured on satellite dishes, those citizens are probably already aware of the dazzling opportunities elsewhere.

As a result, many countries have given up their attempts to remain closed off from the world. They are now opening up to tourists and other visitors. In the past few decades, major countries such as Russia, China, Vietnam, Burma (Myanmar) and many others have become much more open members of the international community. Today, a fifth of the population of Afghanistan have lived abroad for some period of their lives.

Exchange of ideas

It is not just *people* who do the travelling in this new world – *ideas* hitch a ride along with them. Tourists come in with stories of very different worlds, in which people have freedom to act, think and speak. Locals go abroad and are amazed to find that the travellers' tales are true. If people have access to the internet or satellite TV, the stories they hear are confirmed by what they see on-screen.

Trade has the same impact. Once a country is opened up to international trade, its citizens find themselves doing business, and becoming friends, with those in different cultures, and come to understand other ways of living.

This reinforces the pressure on governments to open up even more. People who actually see and experience freedom first-hand understand its enormous power to promote progress and to spread prosperity. They want some of that progress and prosperity for themselves. Technology, trade, migration, tourism and global markets are all ambassadors for a free society.

Growing a free society
Not top-down capitalism

Creating a free society where there was none before is no easy job. New governments and international aid agencies often look for large, spectacular changes, such as replacing the whole adminis-trative bureaucracy, or privatising the big government industries.

Often, this approach is a disaster. With the culture of using power for personal advantage still in place, and no local under-standing of markets and competition, many privatisation initiatives (such as that of Mexico in the late 1980s) have simply transferred state monopolies into the hands of cronies. To the public, this crony capitalism seems no different from the state cronyism that went before. And since reforming the justice system can take decades, such cronyism may even go unchallenged by the courts. So people come to be just as cynical of supposed private-enterprise solutions as they were of the state-control problem. Many may come to believe that only radicals and revolutionaries offer a fresh approach that might benefit the public rather than elites.

Bottom-up drivers of freedom

The 'top-down capitalism' approach fails because it tries to change the appearance of social institutions without changing the fundamental attitudes, actions and incentives that create and support them.

The creativity and progress of a free society grow out of the pattern of legal and moral rules that determine how people live and cooperate freely together. If we can introduce such a pattern of rules of action, and set people free to conduct their own lives within those rules, then the natural energy and ambition of the whole public will drive systemic change.

Suppose, for example, that we make it easy for people to start a new business, to own and run a business with confidence, to have secure ownership of property, to build up productive capital and to trade freely. By doing this, we create rules and incentives that will soon produce economic growth and stimulate systematic social reform. People will start small businesses, learn how business is done, and prosper – achieving not just financial benefit but greater self-confidence too. A more self-confident society will be more able to tackle the big institutional issues such as reforming the bureaucracy and the government industries.

So we should not start at the macro level of trying to reform entire state institutions. We should start at the micro level by unleashing the incentives that will drive systematic change through the whole institutional fabric.[1]

Property rights in action
Property rights in Peru

An interesting example is the *reform of property rights* in Peru, largely driven by the economist Hernando de Soto in the early 1990s. De Soto complained that as a result of bureaucracy and corruption in Peru, it could take nearly a year to register a new business. It was similarly difficult to own property. The result was that millions of small entrepreneurs did not legally own their farm, small business or home. That made it difficult for them to get credit to expand their enterprise. They could not sell their home or business. And they could not use the courts to settle their property or business disputes.

There were in effect two economies in Peru, one within the law and enjoying all the economic benefits of legitimacy and legal protection, and another comprising millions of entrepreneurs trapped in poverty because their homes and businesses did not legally exist. The government lost revenue because it was unable to assess or collect tax on the extralegal small businesses. And with no legal protection available to them, these entrepreneurs were easily exploited by criminals and by the communist Shining Path guerrillas.

The solution that De Soto and others put in place was to

1   I am grateful to Peter Young and Stephen J. Masty of Adam Smith International for their expert insights on this.

eliminate most of the bureaucratic regulation involved in regis-tering a new business, and scrap most of the licences and permits that had to be obtained to run them. There were also land reforms by which more than a million Peruvian families obtained recog-nised land titles for the first time. As a result, the efficiency of small businesses grew, since owners were able to borrow to expand and to buy and sell property. As people acquired capital and savings, housing standards improved and parents started spending more on educating their children.

The reforms were not without criticism. Some people argued that land titling was unfair because it was hard to establish who informally 'owned' what. Others claimed that land titling benefited large-scale squatters over poorer, small-scale ones; that titling ate into the common lands that the poorest farmers depended on; or that titling undermined tenure arrangements that – though informal – actually worked well. Others argued that land reform was no 'silver bullet' and that the biggest obstacles to economic development were the limitations that people's culture imposed on their aspirations.

It is never easy to establish a well-functioning market when none has existed before. It is easy to make fish soup out of an aquarium, but not easy to make an aquarium out of fish soup. Nevertheless, other countries have sought to replicate Peru's reforms, and De Soto himself has advised many, both in Latin America and Africa.

Supporting reforms

But while well-functioning property rights are crucial, other supporting reforms are certainly needed too. For example, there needs to be a functioning *credit and microcredit market*, which onerous regulation and bureaucracy can easily stifle. (An interesting example of microcredit is the Grameen Bank in Bangladesh, which provides small loans to rural businesses – including loans through which landless women entrepreneurs can set up payphone services using wireless telephones.)

There needs also to be a *trustworthy and efficient legal system*, so that people can settle disputes quickly and confidently. We do not have to wait until legislators have thought through and passed specific reforms to the state legal system. The common law, built up from individual cases, is much quicker, and there may be local legal systems already in place with a body of established precedent that accords with local people's sense of justice. But we do need to set out the *basic rules of how businesses operate*, such as ownership structures, personal liability, shareholder rights and bankruptcy arrangements.

We need also to *reduce the regulations* that prevent entry into markets so that new ideas can come through. For example, the rulers of Nepal, a country largely closed to the outside world before the 1950s, rejected outright sale of their telephone system on the grounds that the people would be horrified by the idea of private companies running it. But they agreed to issue new licences that allowed newcomers in. So successful have these new entrants been that Nepal now has an enviable state-of-the-art telephone system.

The more examples there are of small businesses and new market entrants growing, creating jobs, increasing prosperity and improving customer service, the more are people likely to understand the enormous potential of freedom for creating income and wealth. The more support it will gather, the less will people yearn for radical but ultimately coercive alternatives.

Agricultural reforms

An example of the power of property rights in action is agricultural reform in Soviet Russia, China and Vietnam. Their communist governments built agriculture around the communal ownership of land and farm enterprises. The communes controlled the rights to use and work the land and imposed an egalitarian distribution system. But it was a disaster. The communes were vast, unwieldy and bureaucratic. And because individuals had to share the fruits of their efforts with many others, they had little incentive to work harder or more productively.

Though reluctant to give up the principle of communal ownership, China broke with this disastrous Soviet model in the late 1970s. A 'household responsibility system' came in, with families working their own particular patch of land. This restored the link between effort and reward. China's agriculture boomed. Farm output in the early 1980s grew rapidly, with annual increases of nearly 5 per cent for grain, 8 per cent for cotton and 14 per cent for oilseed.[2]

But this early progress did not last. The system was still flawed. Hoping to equalise differences in land quality, the authorities had given families several small patches of land rather than one large one. With each family's effort spread across five or six plots, it was impractical to introduce better methods. Even the paths between the plots took up a large part of the cultivated area. And the distribution system took no account of differences in families' productivity.

So it was decided to leave the technical ownership of land unchanged, but to introduce a land-use rights system – giving

---

2   For details, see Wolfgang Kasper, 'The Sichuan experiment', *Australian Journal of Chinese Affairs*, 7, February 1981, pp. 163–72.

families long-term rights to work land, obtain crops and income from it, and to pass those rights on to others.

Again, this system was not perfect from a free-market or property-rights point of view. The state procurement and price-fixing system undermined farmers' ability to make their own decisions and to enjoy all the fruits of their own labour. Without a real market in land, there was still too little consolidation of small plots. But gradually something like a market in land use opened up.

In the county of Meitan in northern Guizhou, for example, villagers and officials fixed the land-use tenures at twenty years, helping families plan for the long term. Farmers were given the power to bequeath and exchange their tenures and to combine land parcels. And there were incentives to exploit uncultivated land. As a result, more land was brought into cultivation, the quality of land improved because families cared for it better, and modern equipment was introduced. In 1995, the national government urged other villages to follow the Meitan example, and something akin to a property-rights system in land began to spread.

Water rights

Water is another scarce resource that property rights can allocate better than governments. In the dry west of the United States, the threat of drought was once common – not because of the lack of water but because of the highly regulated system for allocating it. Those who first drew water from a stream, for example, had priority over any coming later; but to maintain this right, they had to keep extracting – even if their need for the water was marginal.

In the early 1990s, states such as Montana and Arizona began to allow people to trade their water rights. While there are still many regulations that inhibit this market, it has helped to ensure that water goes to its most valued uses. Since rights to water resources can be bought and sold, marginal users (who can use less water, or use recycled water) now pass on their freshwater extraction rights to those with more urgent needs. Such are the benefits of this system that the water rights market now stretches all over the western United States.

The mechanics of privatisation

State-controlled industries are often monopolies, which give customers no choice. So they can (and do) charge higher prices for inferior goods and services. Even if they are at arm's length from the rulers, being managed by some agency, they are still commonly controlled by the ruling elites or their friends.

The *bonyads* in Iran, for example, are supposedly charitable trusts that control about a fifth of the Iranian economy, in property development, agriculture, manufacturing and shipping. Founded originally by the Shah, they were widely criticised as being not real charities but vehicles for the administration's own patronage and profit. Yet, after the 1979 revolution, the incoming government found them too lucrative to give up. So they persisted, enjoying special tax breaks and government subsidies: indeed, confiscated private property was added to them. They are meant to exist for the benefit of the poor, but their main beneficiaries seem to be those in authority.

Privatising state-run businesses *should* introduce the dynamic effects of private ownership and competition into bureaucratic monopolies, and replace corruption with commercial openness. It can also help return the capital of these industries back to the public. But to achieve all that takes vision, stamina and careful policy formulation.

There is no single mechanism. Privatising state-run businesses is a matter of politics as well as economics. Every industry is different and will require a different approach. Industries are of different kinds and sizes, and have different interest groups blocking reform. So the approach taken for a utility such as water or electricity, on which the whole population depends, will have to be quite different from that for a manufacturing company where comparatively few people are affected.

In the case of smaller enterprises, it may be practical to sell them to a commercial operator, particularly one from abroad which might have fresh ideas and capital. But sales of state companies to foreigners can be controversial.

For larger enterprises, it can be useful to spread the ownership widely among the public by selling shares. This can require a large education exercise, however, as there may be only a primitive stock market and most people will not know what shares are. After the collapse of the Soviet regime, Russia embarked on 'voucher privatisation', which effectively gave the public equal shares in state enterprises. But many people sold these shares cheaply and control ended up in the hands of a new elite class of business 'oligarchs'.

Introducing market principles

It is essential to break down monopolies as part of the privatisation process. Governments may think they would get more revenue from selling businesses with their monopoly privileges intact, but that monopoly power still remains bad for the general public. If a state monopoly is broken down into competing elements, both the government and the people will gain in the long term. The new enterprises will be more robust, dynamic and innovative than their monopoly predecessor.

The 1996 privatisation of Guatemala's telephone system illustrates the importance of competition in the process. There, the telecoms market was opened up to competition *before* the telecom monopoly was privatised. The airwaves were also privatised, effectively creating property rights in the electromagnetic spectrum, which new communications companies could easily buy and use. The result was a huge expansion in competition, bringing greater choice and wider coverage. Prices fell to among the lowest in Latin America, and the number of mobile telephone users increased several hundred times in little more than a decade.[3]

Getting it right

There is plenty of international experience – and expertise – that can help reformers get the politics and the mechanics of privatisation right.

The key thing is that the process should be fully open and that the public should participate in it. Otherwise, the reform will not be generally accepted. For example, some governments in Africa have privatised utility industries such as water and banking by inviting in foreign investors, but not opening up any

---

3   See Wayne A. Leighton, 'Getting privatisation right: a case study', Institute of Economic Affairs blog, London, 2013.

ownership opportunities to the local population. This is not just politically naive, but against the free-society principle of equal treatment.

Furthermore, if ownership is kept narrow rather than spread widely, there remains the danger of privatised industries reverting to control by the cronies of those in government. That will poison the idea of further privatisations and will set back moves to introduce market principles into other government-run sectors. The public need to be reassured that any new structure will serve customers, not corrupt elites. Introducing as much competition as possible, as early as possible, is a good way to guarantee that.

Human services without government

There is a presumption that some public services can be provided only by governments – particularly the 'human' services of health, education and welfare.

Some people say that such essential services are too important to be left to the market. In fact, they are too important to be left to government. When service providers are financed out of taxation, they do not have to please customers to earn their living, as competitive private providers must. The way they boost their budgets is to lobby politicians or to threaten disruption if their demands are not met. Their focus is on government, not on the public.

Private firms face much more competition than government-run services usually do. Often, competing with government services is actually outlawed. So government-sector providers do not have to innovate or even keep their service up to date, because their customers have nowhere else to go.

But however much governments would like to run public services by themselves, people always find ways round their monopoly. There are plenty of examples from around the world where non-government and informal providers supply these important services – and provide them better.

Education without government

Take education, for example. Many people imagine that private education is only for the rich. But a two-year study of India, Ghana, Nigeria and Kenya by education expert Professor James Tooley found the opposite. In the poorest areas of these countries, most schoolchildren were attending non-government schools. In the poorest parts of Hyderabad, Accra and Lagos, only a third or fewer schools were government schools. Two-thirds or more of schoolchildren went to private schools, many of them unofficial ones not recognised by the government. Private owners ran most of these non-government schools. Very few received charitable support and none received state funding – parental fees, often very low, were their sole income.[4]

Even so, Tooley found that achievement was considerably higher in the private schools. In Hyderabad, average mathematics scores were around a fifth higher than in government schools – despite the fact that teacher salary costs in the private sector were between a half and a quarter of those in the government sector. Other standards were similarly higher. Tooley found teachers in government schools asleep at their desks. And teacher absenteeism was worse in the government schools. The private schools

---

4   See James Tooley, *The Beautiful Tree: A Personal Journey into How the World's Poorest People Are Educating Themselves*, Cato Institute, Washington, DC, 2009.

had better provision of blackboards, playgrounds, desks, drinking water and toilets. (Only half of government schools provided toilets, compared to 96 per cent or more of the private schools.) Pupil–teacher ratios were nearly half those of the government schools.

Governments seem unaware of the huge importance of private education in poor areas. The Chinese government records only 44 private schools in the mountain province of Gansu, though Tooley's researchers found 696 of them, 593 of which served 61,000 children in the most remote villages. The vast majority were run by parents and villagers. They thrived despite average incomes in Gansu being around only $150 a year. Even in Kibera, Kenya – the largest slum in sub-Saharan Africa, with a population of around 750,000 – Tooley found 76 private schools, enrolling 12,000 students.

Plainly, even in some of the world's poorest places, private initiative can and does deliver education to a higher standard than the state. And its cost is low enough to make it affordable to poor families. Government does not seem to be needed in education at all.

It is no wonder that rich countries, which often have extensive government-run schools programmes, are keen to bring some of this competition and parental choice into education. In 1991, Sweden introduced a new system by which the government continued to pay the basic costs of schooling, but private non-profit and for-profit groups could set up their own schools to capture that funding, on the basis of the number of pupils they could attract. Even critics such as the teachers' unions which originally opposed this reform now support it, such has been the impact on the efficiency, innovation and quality of the thousand-plus new schools that have started up – particularly in the most difficult and poorest areas. Now other countries are introducing the same model.

Healthcare without government

Healthcare is another important service that in many countries is dominated by government provision – often protected against competitors by legal privileges, tax-funded subsidies and regulation. Again, this focuses the attention of state providers on getting more money and greater privileges out of the government, rather than providing a good service to patients.

The United States is often criticised for the high cost of its supposedly 'free-market' healthcare system. It is certainly costly; but in fact it is one of the most regulated systems in the world, and its per-capita government spending on healthcare is the third highest in the world (behind Norway and Luxembourg). Tax and regulatory rules tie the supply of health insurance to workplaces – which leaves people uninsured when they are between jobs. Meanwhile employees (encouraged by doctors) demand tests and treatment they do not really need because the cost is borne by their employers rather than themselves. Regulations also dictate what must be included in a medical insurance contract and how it can be sold (for example, limiting insurers to operating only in their home state, making them unable to secure economies of scale). Similarly, medical practice is governed by licensing requirements that are largely designed by the doctors themselves – allowing the profession to restrict the supply of doctors and keep their remuneration high. All of this (and more) regulation adds to the cost of US healthcare.

By contrast, Singapore – a small country that is actually richer than the USA – spends about a sixth of America's per-capita expenditure on government-sponsored health programmes. It requires only that families save about a fifth of their income for future healthcare, retirement and housing costs (though there is a government-funded programme for catastrophic medical needs). The fact that people are saving their own money in their own health savings account makes them keen to get good value, and private doctors and clinics compete for their custom.

In Switzerland, there is no government-run insurance: people buy insurance and medical services from private providers. The government's role is limited to giving subsidies – not to providers, but to patients who cannot afford basic healthcare themselves. So again, unlike Americans, Swiss citizens are keen to get value for money for what they spend on healthcare. Many Europeans regard Switzerland's largely free-market system as probably the best healthcare system in the world.

Welfare without government

The best form of welfare for a poor person is to have a paying job. But government-run welfare schemes destroy jobs. In much of Europe, 'social insurance' is funded by a specific tax on those in work, which raises costs for employers and makes them more reluctant to hire new workers. That means more people drawing unemployment benefit, which then requires further tax increases to fund, leading to even less hiring. It is a downward spiral.

Sweden was a free, low-tax and prosperous country until the mid-twentieth century. Then for two decades from 1970 it began to impose very high taxes in order to finance its comprehensive welfare programmes. (Indeed, in 1976 one Swedish author complained that her marginal tax rate had reached 102 per cent!) These high taxes were a major disincentive on work and enterprise. They condemned Sweden to two decades of low growth, until the policy began to be reversed in the 1990s.

Free countries tend to be richer; and richer countries tend to spend more on charitable support of the needy. This is morally healthier than governments taking money from people through taxation to spend on welfare programmes of their own design – and not just because governments tend to give the benefits to their friends and impose the tax on their enemies. Genuine charity is a voluntary transfer from one person to another, not a forced one.

Another problem with government welfare programmes is the way they create a culture of dependency. Being large, and run by public servants, they necessarily operate on the basis of rules, rather than on a personal evaluation of the needs and potential of the beneficiaries, as genuine charity does. That encourages people to 'game' the rules to ensure they qualify. Sometimes, poor families deliberately worsen their circumstances in order to qualify for higher benefits – the opposite of what we want to achieve. In the oldest and largest welfare-state countries such as the United Kingdom, officials are now seeing third-generation dependency – families living on benefits whose parents and grandparents did the same before them.

Self-help, backed by private charity, is a more humane, motivating and effective alternative. The UK had a thriving system of working-class welfare before the 1940s, when the welfare state swept it away. These were the friendly societies, to which members would make weekly contributions in return for benefits such as unemployment pay, medical insurance and even funeral expenses. They usually focused on particular occupations, so they could cater for the special needs of those workers. Millions of families, poorer families in particular, chose to be members of one of these bodies. Welfare for all, without government, is certainly achievable.

Reviving the philanthropic sector

Many people who live in countries with advanced state welfare systems argue that private charity and philanthropy could not possibly replace the generosity of tax-funded social benefits and pensions. It is very easy for governments to be 'generous' with other people's money, of course, and there is every incentive for politicians to promise extravagant benefits now, knowing that generations yet unborn will end up paying for them. That itself would be a good reason to keep politicians out of social welfare. But in addition, if state benefits are high, there is less incentive for families to provide for themselves and for individuals to seek work rather than live on benefits – all the more so if those in work have to pay high taxes in order to fund the welfare system. Though this is well intentioned, the end result is to drain people of hope and ambition and condemn them to a life of dependency.

Countries that wish to move in the direction of freedom should start by breaking down their huge state welfare systems into much smaller and more local systems. They can even be 'individuated' into some kind of personal account. That can help make families realise their own responsibilities, and to understand that they are being supported by real taxpayers, not some diffuse 'system'. And breaking down the system like this allows it to be managed more efficiently, by private-sector providers.

An example is the Chilean pension system. In 1981, the country split its failing and unfair state pension system into personal accounts. Workers were obliged to save towards their retirement, but they could choose between several private providers to manage their funds. The system promoted personal responsibility in savings, produced better returns for workers, and has since been copied in a number of countries in several continents.

Another example is Singapore's system of health savings accounts (see above), which puts considerable responsibility on individuals and families, encouraging people to provide for their own healthcare and other needs. The United Kingdom's old friendly societies are another model that could easily be recreated by splitting state benefits into personal, private accounts.

When the failing apparatus of state support is reformed in such ways, there are greater incentives for individuals to seek work and to rely on their own efforts and the support of their families, rather than on the state. There will still be a need for private charity and philanthropy, but it will be of more manageable proportions. And, as we have seen, freedom and low taxes are a good way to give people both the will and the wealth to be generous, a motive that a big state and high taxes extinguish.

Globalisation and trade

The benefits of globalisation

Like Nepal, many countries are concerned about how increasingly globalised markets will affect them. But much of the concern is misplaced, and the positive gains from globalisation and trade are substantial.

Thanks to the mechanism of market prices, we can now trade

directly and indirectly with people from all over the world. The clothes we wear, the food we eat, the equipment in our homes, offices and factories, are all the products of a surprisingly large number of distant countries.

But the globalisation of markets works both ways. It does not just enable rich countries to buy things from across the entire world. It also enables people in once-remote countries to improve their own prospects by plugging into the international markets for their product. What crops, for example, should a local farmer grow? Previously, the only sources of information on crop prices were local merchants or state agencies, who of course have interests of their own. Local prices could fluctuate widely, depending on factors such as the weather. And local markets were not always well organised. Today, the farmer can take out a mobile phone and check any number of websites that list market prices – including future price offers – for almost any crop, in countless markets across the world. Farmers anywhere can now sell into an organised, international market, at much more predictable prices.

Opening up New Zealand

New Zealand is an example of a country that was turned around by abandoning regulations on commerce and trade. In the early 1980s, it was in a very depressed and difficult economic situation owing largely to such regulation. But, starting in 1984, it abandoned protectionism and liberalised its international trade, opening its markets to world competition. Subsidies to industry and agriculture were eliminated. Domestic markets were deregulated, including the highly regulated labour market: trade union membership was made voluntary and contracts were left to negotiation between workers and bosses.

The dire predictions from lobbyists, academics, religious leaders and union officials – that this deregulation would create a 'sweatshop economy' – were all proved wrong. Average wages rose. Wage contracts were settled more quickly. Strike action fell to near zero. Unemployment fell – and fell fastest among Maori, immigrants and other poor or disadvantaged groups. New Zealand became one of the world's most free and competitive countries.[5]

Cultural identity

Some people worry that the globalisation of markets could rob countries of their unique identity and culture. In particular, the spread of American brands raises concerns that once-distinctive countries will start to look depressingly similar, that Western goods and attitudes will swamp those of other places, and that the world's highest cultures will be overwhelmed by some lowest common denominator.

Certainly, economic and social cultures are changing. Products that were once unique to a particular country are now found on the high streets of all. That does not mean that choice and variety are disappearing. On the contrary, it means that the people of every country now have far more choice than they ever did before. Citizens of the United Kingdom, for example, no longer have to endure the bland and overcooked food for which their country was once famous. They can now find restaurants, takeaway shops and supermarkets selling Indian, Vietnamese,

5   For an outline by the architect of these reforms, see Roger Douglas, *Toward Prosperity*, David Bateman, Auckland, NZ, 1987.

Latin American, Iranian, Mongolian, Polish and countless other varieties of food. And others across the world now enjoy the same sort of choices – choices that were once limited to the lucky few who were rich enough to travel. It is not that cultures are being lost; rather, they are spreading such that everyone can enjoy them.

Cultures never remain static and unchanging, as those who want to defend them from globalisation imply. A country's culture changes all the time, and the more vivid and alive a culture is, the more new cultural ideas it generates and the more it changes. The art, music, literature, lifestyles, tastes and fashions of the most vibrant countries today would be quite unfamiliar to those who lived in them just a century ago.

Cultures gain from being exposed to other cultures, allowing people to pick the elements most suited to their own lives and time. Through international trade we get to see and understand cultural elements from abroad that we find useful to adapt into our own. But this process of change was going on long before anyone talked about globalisation.

And much of the change that we most regret, the loss of the most colourful parts of our culture, is not due to any cultural imperialism from abroad but to the simple effects of modernisation. Ancient ceremonies, customs and national dress disappear, not because of globalisation, but because life itself changes. Festivals that once marked particular seasons were important to farming communities, but now have very little resonance in a world where half of us live in cities.[6]

Perhaps it is just as well that cultures change. Many of the world's

---

6   For these points, see Mario Vargas Llosa, 'The culture of liberty', in Tom G. Palmer, *The Morality of Capitalism*, Students for Liberty and Atlas Foundation, Arlington, VA, 2011.

> **Question: Aren't rich countries grabbing too much of the world's wealth?**
>
> No. Wealth is something you *create*, through skill, enterprise, energy, effort, organisation and investment. Rich countries certainly consume wealth, but they create it too. And not just for themselves: they discover and develop vital products and processes that improve the lives of everyone, particularly the lives of some of the poorest people on the planet.
>
> Advances in medicine, for example, are helping to eradicate some of the world's most crippling diseases such as tuberculosis and malaria. Genetic technology is helping to boost both the yields and the pest-resistance of rice and other staple crops. New materials are making buildings cheaper and safer.
>
> There is no fixed supply of wealth, with the rich countries grabbing an unfair share. On the contrary, expertise from the rich countries is creating new opportunities for others.

cultures were forced on their peoples by occupying powers, and much of the culture of the least-free countries is actually damaging. We should welcome the fact that improved travel and wider questioning have made it hard for countries to maintain a culture in which some groups are routinely abused, suppressed or discriminated against.

The importance of peace

Adam Smith once wrote: 'Little else is requisite to carry a state to the highest degree of opulence from the lowest barbarism but peace, easy taxes and a tolerable administration of justice...'[7]

---

7   Lecture in 1755, quoted in Dugald Stewart, *Account of the Life and Writings of Adam Smith LLD*, Section IV, 25.

Peace at home and abroad is definitely a requirement for a flourishing free economy. People will not invest in enterprises and build up productive capital if they believe their wealth is likely to be stolen by warring militias or invading armies. And countries whose citizens are engaged in trade with those in other countries are much less likely to seek conflict with them. In the words attributed to the nineteenth-century French economist and politician Frédéric Bastiat: 'If goods do not cross borders, armies will.'[8]

The benefits of peace are both economic and cultural. Peace allows effort and resources to be focused on productive activities rather than destructive ones. It provides the conditions for capital creation and a prospering free economy. It allows people to map out a future for themselves and their families. It gives them the time, wealth and confidence to engage in cultural and educational pursuits. And peace allows the free movement of people, goods and ideas – spreading understanding, prosperity and innovation.

Another of Adam Smith's insights was that we do not have to make other countries poor in order to become rich ourselves. It is better for us if our customers are rich rather than poor.[9] Likewise, to be strong, we do not have to make others weak. Both sides gain from the benefits of peace.

Peace must, from time to time, be fought for. Property and people must be defended. And marshalling the necessary resources may require (limited) government involvement. But governments that grow large often become militaristic too

---

8   There is no evidence that Bastiat actually said these words, but they sum up his point of view. See Frédéric Bastiat, *Bastiat's 'The Law'*, Institute of Economic Affairs, London, 2001 [1850].

9   'As a rich man is likely to be a better customer to the industrious people of his neighbourhood than a poor, so likewise is a rich nation.' Adam Smith, *The Wealth of Nations*, 1776, Book IV, ch. III, Part II.

– perhaps seeking to conceal the lack of prosperity and freedom by suggesting that the security of the nation requires sacrifice, unity of purpose and military strength. People in free societies are no less loyal to their countries; but their commitment is to an open and free society and to their family, friends, customers and voluntary associations – not to a dictator, a flag or some nationalist dream.

Some people imagine that the way to peace is to set up some kind of supranational world government. While it is useful to have international forums in which differences can be aired and potential conflicts defused, we should not suppose that a world government would be any better than our existing national ones. Given its vast scale, and even greater distance from the public, its tendency to expand and abuse its power would be all the greater. Nor could anyone escape that abuse by moving to another part of the world. No, the best way to promote peace is to make governments smaller, not larger, and to rely instead on the natural tendency of human beings to cooperate peacefully and better their mutual condition.

9 THE ARGUMENT IN BRIEF

The case for freedom

Freedom creates prosperity. Societies that have embraced freedom have made themselves rich. Those that have not have remained poor.

But a free society is superior in non-material ways too. It operates on the basis of mutual trust and cooperation between individuals, not on the basis of power and coercion. Its citizens share deep cultural, personal and moral ties. They accept rules of interpersonal behaviour voluntarily, for their mutual benefit, not because these rules are imposed on them. Their governments have the consent of the governed, and are themselves governed by rules to prevent them exploiting their authority.

A free society unleashes human talent, invention and innovation. That enables it to create wealth where none existed before. People in a free society do not become rich by exploiting others, as the elites of less-free countries do. They cannot become rich by making others poorer. They become rich only by providing others with what they want and making other people's lives better.

Limited government

Most people agree that government is needed for purposes such as delivering justice and deciding on things that individuals cannot decide alone. But nearly everyone agrees that government power must be limited. The government of a free society exists to prevent harm being done to its citizens. It maintains and enforces justice – the natural rules that enable human beings to cooperate peacefully together.

The government of a free society is constrained by the rule of law. Its laws apply to everyone equally. Its leaders cannot plunder citizens for their own benefit, grant favours to their friends, or use their power against their enemies. Their powers and their time in office are both limited in order to reduce the corruption that comes with authority. Democratic institutions such as free and open elections, the right to free speech, term limits on representatives and constitutional rules all maintain limits on the powers of political leaders.

Greater equality

The chief beneficiaries of the economic dynamism of free societies are the poor. Free societies are economically more equal than non-free societies. The poor in the most-free societies enjoy luxuries that were undreamed of just a few years ago, luxuries available only to the ruling elites of non-free countries.

A free society does not try to impose material equality. It recognises that the attempt to equalise wealth or income is counterproductive. It destroys the incentives for self-improvement, hard work and enterprise. It discourages people from building up the capital that boosts the productivity of the whole society. It prevents individuals from creating new wealth and new value.

But free societies enjoy even more important equalities that often do not exist in non-free societies. People's moral equality is recognised: every human life is considered of value and worth protecting. There is equality before the law: judgements depend on the facts of the case, not on who you are. Citizens have political equality: they are all entitled to vote, stand in elections and express their political views, no matter how uncomfortable that is for the authorities. And they have equality of opportunity: people face no discrimination in work or education and can improve themselves regardless of their race, religion, ethnicity or any other characteristic.

A free economy

A free society gives people freedom to make their own economic choices, just as it leaves them free to make their own social and personal choices. People in a free society create value through voluntary exchange. Free exchange makes both sides better off: they would not do it otherwise.

Individuals prosper by cooperating with others and supplying the products they want – and getting something that they want in return. The prospect of gain encourages entrepreneurs to seek out what others want and to supply it. Prices communicate information about shortages and surpluses, telling everyone what needs to be produced and what needs to be conserved. In this way, time, skill, effort, capital and other resources are drawn automatically to where demand is urgent and steered away from less important uses. It does not need government to tell people what to do.

To function, a free economy needs only an accepted framework of rules about how people cooperate together. These include rules about the ownership and transfer of property, and rules of contract under which agreements are honoured. Private property is necessary if people are to build up businesses and exchange goods. But it is also essential if other freedoms are to be respected. If the authorities control all property, political action and open debate become impossible.

Justice and the rule of law

Justice is not something that can be dictated by legislators. The rules of justice are a part of human nature – a vital part of us which helps to promote peaceful cooperation between individuals.

People in a free society have a right to this natural justice by virtue of their humanity. Natural justice holds that laws must be clear and certain, that they treat people equally, that they do not require the impossible, that they are not retrospective, and that penalties are predictable and commensurate to the offence. There must be due process of law in all cases, with fair trials and no lengthy detention without trial. People accused of offences must be treated as innocent until proved guilty, and individuals must not be harassed by being prosecuted several times for the same offence. Such principles are accepted by almost everyone, regardless of their country, culture, race or religion.

To guarantee this natural justice and uphold the rule of law requires a properly independent judiciary that cannot be influenced by political leaders. The police, similarly, must be independent. Bribes and corruption cannot be tolerated among the police and judiciary if freedom is to prevail.

The spontaneous society

A free society is a spontaneous society. It builds up from the actions of individuals, following the rules that promote peaceful cooperation. It is not imposed from above by political authorities.

People do not have to agree on everything in order to cooperate to mutual advantage. Those exchanging goods need agree only on price. But for that cooperation to be most fruitful, individuals must tolerate the views and actions of others. A free society allows individuals or governments to interfere with others only to prevent actual harm being done. Limiting people's freedom because we find their behaviour disagreeable or offensive removes any barrier against everyone's freedom being curtailed by those who think themselves morally superior.

Tolerating other people's ideas and lifestyles benefits society. Truth is not always obvious; it emerges in the battle of ideas. We cannot trust censors to suppress only wrong ideas. They may mistakenly suppress ideas and ways of acting that would greatly benefit society in the future.

A world of freedom

It is becoming more difficult for authoritarian governments to hide their actions from the rest of the world. As a result, more and more countries are opening up to trade and tourism, and new ideas are spreading. More people see the benefits of economic and social freedom, and are demanding them.

It is hard to create the morality and institutions of a free society where freedom does not exist. Rather than trying to impose them wholesale, it is better to start at the micro level, creating the conditions that allow people to act freely and build up a free society through their actions. A key part of this is to institute property rights, so that people can build up businesses and trade with confidence that their property will not be confiscated.

Reforms should deliver genuine economic freedom, not crony capitalism. Too many governments that have claimed to be privatising state industries have in fact merely transferred their ownership to friends and relatives. The whole population needs to be engaged in the process of economic reform if there is to be real change.

Countries do not lose from opening up to international trade. Protecting domestic producers against competition simply means higher prices and lower quality for domestic consumers. Being part of the international trade community gives local entrepreneurs new markets and opportunities. The opening up of trade over the last three decades has lifted more than a billion people out of abject poverty. Freedom is truly one of the most benign and productive forces in human history.

SELECT BIBLIOGRAPHY

Ashford, N. (2003), *Principles for a Free Society*, Stockholm: Jarl Hjalmarson Foundation. Thorough, short exposition of the principles on which a free society and free economy are built.

Bastiat, F. (2001 [1850]), *Bastiat's 'The Law'*, London: Institute of Economic Affairs. Classic statement of liberal ideas from the French politician and political thinker.

Benn, E. (1964), *Why Freedom Works*, London: Sir Ernest Benn Ltd. Dated but enlightening defence of free markets by a leading UK businessman.

Butler, E. (2009), *The Best Book on the Market: How to Stop Worrying and Love the Free Economy*, Oxford: Capstone Books. Simple outline of how markets and trade really work.

Butler, E. (2012), *Public Choice – a Primer*, London: Institute of Economic Affairs. Simple explanation of government failure and the problems of self-interest in democratic systems.

Butler, E. (2012), *Friedrich Hayek: The Ideas and Influence of the Libertarian Economist*, Petersfield: Harriman House. Easy introduction to the liberal political scientist who developed much of the modern thinking on the spontaneous society.

Friedman, M. with R. Friedman (1962), *Capitalism and Freedom*, Chicago, IL: University of Chicago Press. Classic outline of the case for a free society and free economy by the US Nobel laureate in Economics.

Friedman, M. and R. Friedman (1980), *Free to Choose*, New York: Harcourt Brace Jovanovich. Engaging case for the free society, based on the television series of the same name.

Hayek, F. A. (1944), *The Road to Serfdom*, London: Routledge. Classic wartime exposition of the dangers of central planning and unrestrained governments.

Hayek, F. A. (1960), *The Constitution of Liberty*, London: Routledge. Large book tracing the origins of liberal ideas and the principles on which a free society must be founded.

Meadowcroft, J. (ed.) (2008), *Prohibitions*, London: Institute of Economic Affairs. Powerful set of arguments against government controls on many different lifestyle choices.

Mill, J. S. (1859), *On Liberty*, in J. S. Mill (2008), *On Liberty and Other Essays*, Oxford: Oxford University Press. *On Liberty* is a classic text on the case for freedom, the no-harm principle, limited government, natural justice and tolerance.

Norberg, J. (2003), *In Defense of Global Capitalism*, Washington, DC: Cato Institute. An instructive survey of the benefits delivered, to the poor in particular, by international capitalism.

Palmer, T. G. (ed.) (2011), *The Morality of Capitalism*, Arlington, VA: Students for Liberty and Atlas Foundation. Interesting collection of essays on morality, cooperation, equality, progress, globalisation and culture.

Pirie, M. (2008), *Freedom 101*, London: Adam Smith Institute. One hundred and one arguments against the free economy, knocked down in a page each.

Wellings, R. (ed.) (2009), *A Beginner's Guide to Liberty*, London: Adam Smith Research Trust. Straightforward explanations of markets, property rights, liberty, government failure, prohibitions and welfare without the state.

ABOUT THE IEA

The Institute is a research and educational charity (No. CC 235 351), limited by guarantee. Its mission is to improve understanding of the fundamental institutions of a free society by analysing and expounding the role of markets in solving economic and social problems.

The IEA achieves its mission by:

- a high-quality publishing programme
- conferences, seminars, lectures and other events
- outreach to school and college students
- brokering media introductions and appearances

The IEA, which was established in 1955 by the late Sir Antony Fisher, is an educational charity, not a political organisation. It is independent of any political party or group and does not carry on activities intended to affect support for any political party or candidate in any election or referendum, or at any other time. It is financed by sales of publications, conference fees and voluntary donations.

In addition to its main series of publications the IEA also publishes a termly journal, *Economic Affairs*.

The IEA is aided in its work by a distinguished international Academic Advisory Council and an eminent panel of Honorary Fellows. Together with other academics, they review prospective IEA publications, their comments being passed on anonymously to authors. All IEA papers are therefore subject to the same rigorous independent refereeing process as used by leading academic journals.

IEA publications enjoy widespread classroom use and course adoptions in schools and universities. They are also sold throughout the world and often translated/reprinted.

Since 1974 the IEA has helped to create a worldwide network of 100 similar institutions in over 70 countries. They are all independent but share the IEA's mission.

Views expressed in the IEA's publications are those of the authors, not those of the Institute (which has no corporate view), its Managing Trustees, Academic Advisory Council members or senior staff.

Members of the Institute's Academic Advisory Council, Honorary Fellows, Trustees and Staff are listed on the following page.

The Institute gratefully acknowledges financial support for its publications programme and other work from a generous benefaction by the late Alec and Beryl Warren.

Other papers recently published by the IEA include:

Taxation and Red Tape
The Cost to British Business of Complying with the UK Tax System
Francis Chittenden, Hilary Foster & Brian Sloan
Research Monograph 64; ISBN 978 0 255 36612 0; £12.50

Ludwig von Mises – A Primer
Eamonn Butler
Occasional Paper 143; ISBN 978 0 255 36629 8; £7.50

Does Britain Need a Financial Regulator?
Statutory Regulation, Private Regulation and Financial Markets
Terry Arthur & Philip Booth
Hobart Paper 169; ISBN 978 0 255 36593 2; £12.50

Hayek's *The Constitution of Liberty*
An Account of Its Argument
Eugene F. Miller
Occasional Paper 144; ISBN 978 0 255 36637 3; £12.50

Fair Trade Without the Froth
A Dispassionate Economic Analysis of 'Fair Trade'
Sushil Mohan
Hobart Paper 170; ISBN 978 0 255 36645 8; £10.00

A New Understanding of Poverty
Poverty Measurement and Policy Implications
Kristian Niemietz
Research Monograph 65; ISBN 978 0 255 36638 0; £12.50

The Challenge of Immigration
A Radical Solution
Gary S. Becker
Occasional Paper 145; ISBN 978 0 255 36613 7; £7.50

Sharper Axes, Lower Taxes
Big Steps to a Smaller State
Edited by Philip Booth
Hobart Paperback 38; ISBN 978 0 255 36648 9; £12.50

Self-employment, Small Firms and Enterprise
Peter Urwin
Research Monograph 66; ISBN 978 0 255 36610 6; £12.50

Crises of Governments
The Ongoing Global Financial Crisis and Recession
Robert Barro
Occasional Paper 146; ISBN 978 0 255 36657 1; £7.50

... and the Pursuit of Happiness
Wellbeing and the Role of Government
Edited by Philip Booth
Readings 64; ISBN 978 0 255 36656 4; £12.50

Public Choice – A Primer
Eamonn Butler
Occasional Paper 147; ISBN 978 0 255 36650 2; £10.00

The Profit Motive in Education: Continuing the Revolution
Edited by James B. Stanfield
Readings 65; ISBN 978 0 255 36646 5; £12.50

Which Road Ahead – Government or Market?
Oliver Knipping & Richard Wellings
Hobart Paper 171; ISBN 978 0 255 36619 9; £10.00

The Future of the Commons
Beyond Market Failure and Government Regulation
Elinor Ostrom et al.
Occasional Paper 148; ISBN 978 0 255 36653 3; £10.00

Redefining the Poverty Debate
Why a War on Markets is No Substitute for a War on Poverty
Kristian Niemietz
Research Monograph 67; ISBN 978 0 255 36652 6; £12.50

The Euro – the Beginning, the Middle ... and the End?
Edited by Philip Booth
Hobart Paperback 39; ISBN 978 0 255 36680 9; £12.50

The Shadow Economy
Friedrich Schneider & Colin C. Williams
Hobart Paper 172; ISBN 978 0 255 36674 8; £12.50

Quack Policy
Abusing Science in the Cause of Paternalism
Jamie Whyte
Hobart Paper 173; ISBN 978 0 255 36673 1; £10.00

Other IEA publications

Comprehensive information on other publications and the wider work of the IEA can be found at www.iea.org.uk. To order any publication please see below.

Personal customers

Orders from personal customers should be directed to the IEA:
Clare Rusbridge
IEA
2 Lord North Street
FREEPOST LON10168
London SW1P 3YZ
Tel: 020 7799 8907. Fax: 020 7799 2137
Email: crusbridge@iea.org.uk

Trade customers

All orders from the book trade should be directed to the IEA's distributor:
Gazelle Book Services Ltd (IEA Orders)
FREEPOST RLYS-EAHU-YSCZ
White Cross Mills
Hightown
Lancaster LA1 4XS
Tel: 01524 68765. Fax: 01524 53232
Email: sales@gazellebooks.co.uk

IEA subscriptions

The IEA also offers a subscription service to its publications. For a single annual payment (currently £42.00 in the UK), subscribers receive every monograph the IEA publishes. For more information please contact:
Clare Rusbridge
Subscriptions
IEA
2 Lord North Street
FREEPOST LON10168
London SW1P 3YZ
Tel: 020 7799 8907. Fax: 020 7799 2137
Email: crusbridge@iea.org.uk